ARCADIAN THAMES

MAVIS BATEY

KIM WILKIE

HENRIETTA BUTTERY

DAVID LAMBERT

BARN • ELMS

ARCADIAN THAMES

THE RIVER LANDSCAPE FROM
HAMPTON TO KEW

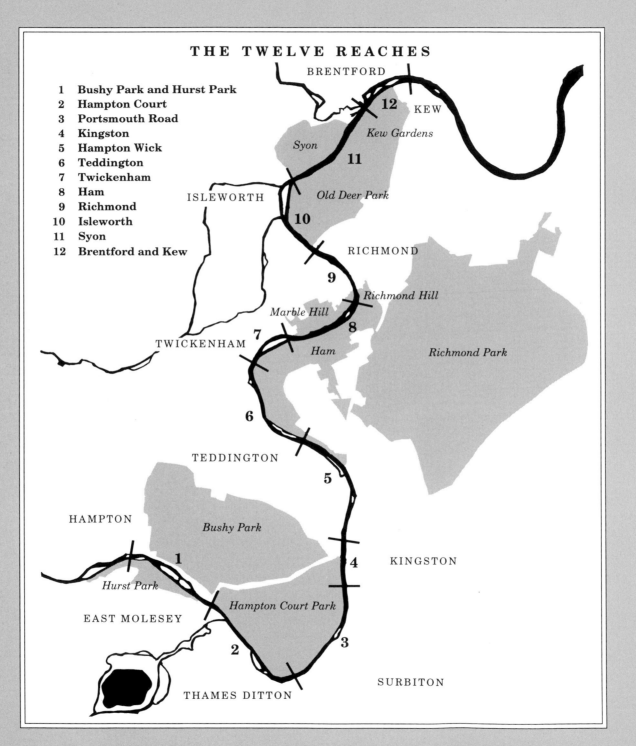

THE TWELVE REACHES

1 **Bushy Park and Hurst Park**
2 **Hampton Court**
3 **Portsmouth Road**
4 **Kingston**
5 **Hampton Wick**
6 **Teddington**
7 **Twickenham**
8 **Ham**
9 **Richmond**
10 **Isleworth**
11 **Syon**
12 **Brentford and Kew**

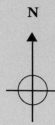

N

BRENTFORD

KEW

Syon

Kew Gardens

12

11

ISLEWORTH

Old Deer Park

10

RICHMOND

9

Richmond Hill

Marble Hill

8

Ham

TWICKENHAM

7

Richmond Park

6

TEDDINGTON

5

HAMPTON

Bushy Park

4

KINGSTON

1

Hurst Park

Hampton Court Park

EAST MOLESEY

3

2

SURBITON

THAMES DITTON

CONTENTS

1. *The Thames at Isleworth* painted by J.M.W. Turner (1805, detail). Tate Gallery, London

FOREWORD

This book stems directly from *The Thames Landscape Strategy: Hampton to Kew* launched by the Minister for Local Government and Planning on 14 June 1994. The Strategy itself is a unique forward-looking project, funded by the Countryside Commission, English Heritage and the Royal Fine Art Commission Trust, to conserve the remarkable eleven mile stretch of the river from Hampton to Kew. The vision for the river, conceived by Kim Wilkie, originated from his ideas about the network of vistas along and across the river produced for the Royal Fine Art Commission's *Thames Connections* exhibition in 1991. Stimulated by the interest of local groups the project evolved into a full study of the dynamic river landscape from Hampton to Kew, with its palaces, parks, villas and working communities. *The Thames Landscape Strategy* analyses the character of the landscape and proposes integrated policies, projects and landscape management practices endorsed by the relevant national agencies, local planning authorities and landowners.

Man's imprint on the landscape for settlement, survival, profit and pleasure – the Thames 'observables' – are integral to the present assessment of the character of the landscape. Historical research following the twelve visual reaches of the river from Hampton to Kew has added a new dimension to local histories, which are usually limited to parish boundaries, and to county histories, which, of necessity, divide along the Thames into the Surrey south bank and the Middlesex north. The Strategy likewise considers the study area regardless of local authority boundaries and brings together landscape, history and nature conservation to produce a policy for the river as a whole. The innovative partnership of environmental agencies which has enabled the original vision to become reality will ensure that the legacy of the past is managed for the future.

By focusing on the historical contributions of the Garden History Society together with the landscape and ecological assessments of the report, and by introducing wide-ranging well-illustrated essays on subjects relating to the river landscape, it is hoped that *Arcadian Thames* will bring *The Thames Landscape Strategy* to wider notice.

Mavis Batey, Henrietta Buttery, David Lambert, Kim Wilkie

2. The unveiling of the Brentford Monument on 12 May 1909. Gunnersbury Park Museum

INTRODUCTION

T HE THAMES from Hampton to Kew has seen great changes in its landscape and in its patterns of human settlement ranging from prehistoric hunters to working communities. In its suburban relationship to London it has also changed considerably from being an out-of-town retreat for royalty, courtiers and a cultural élite to being a haven for commuters and weekend leisure. For the purpose of this study the story begins half a million years ago when the Thames carved out its present course. The river originally flowed through the Vale of St Albans, but when this became blocked by a great glacier the river was diverted in a southerly direction to its present course.

Around 300,000 BC, after a succession of cold and warm phases, three gravel Thames terraces were formed at different levels where the ice sheets ended. The gravel terraces were in some places capped with wind-borne 'brickearth' soil, which is found between Strawberry Hill and Marble Hill, in limited quantities on the opposite bank around Ham House, and at Isleworth and Brentford. Human occupation in the area is known at this time through finds of hand-axes belonging to hunter food-gatherers who had arrived from the warmer south of the Continent in pursuit of migratory herds. The excavated bones of the animals they hunted belong to successive warm and cold periods, indicating that at times there were elephants and hippopotami drinking or wallowing in the Thames and in icy periods reindeer and mammoth in the area.

The fluctuations in the warm and cold periods lasted until about 100,000 BC, and each change affected the flow of the river. The extra water caused by a melt from a glacial period would increase the strength of the Thames, cutting a deeper channel. When the climate became warmer, the river would slow. As this process repeated itself, each previous floodplain was left as a terrace. The landscape gradually acquired the meanders of the 'fair-winding' Thames which were to be so favoured by picturesque artists, landscape designers and, more practically, by the earlier farmer settlers.

There was a gradual thaw from 13,000 BC, and no further glacial periods. The sea levels rose and by 6000 BC Britain was finally cut off from the Continent, giving it an identity of its own. There was a changing relationship between man and the landscape as conditions became more suitable for permanent settlement, agriculture and the domestication of sheep and cattle. The Thames was always the obvious route for traders and colonisers linking Britain through the Rhine with Europe. The first

3. *The Thames at Richmond with the Old Royal Palace* painted by an
artist of the Flemish School in the early seventeenth century (detail).
Fitzwilliam Museum, Cambridge

arrivals in the recolonisation after the landbridge with Europe was broken probably came from Northern France and Belgium around 4000 BC. The last wave of immigration, shortly before the coming of the Romans, was by the Belgae, whom Julius Caesar said were a Celtic people who 'came to plunder and stayed to till'.

The tradition that Caesar crossed the Thames in the area in 54 BC is discussed in the description of the Brentford reach *(page 123)*. With Caesar we reach the period of written history and have a record of the names of the tribes and some of the Celtic chiefs he encountered. The early nomadic hunters had only been grouped in small bands but settled farming led to co-operative organisation and eventually to a tribal system. We know from Caesar's history that the Thames formed a natural tribal physical barrier and that when he crossed the ford from the southern bank he was confronted by Cassivellaunus, who ruled what became Saxon Middlesex.

The Roman order finally collapsed in the early part of the 5th century and 100 years later the East Saxons began to colonise the area north of the Thames, which soon after admitted the supremacy of Mercia. Being situated between the East and West Saxons, it became known as Middlesex, the earliest record of which is in a Saxon charter of 704. The Saxons developed territorial rather than tribal boundaries and introduced the idea of kingship and a feudal society. A chain of contiguous Anglo-Saxon kingships grew up which was the beginning of our shire system. It was the advanced administrative system instituted by the Saxons that made the Norman Domesday survey possible in 1086.

In Saxon times the recognisable pattern of the village settlement of the area from Hampton to Kew emerges. The Saxon place names are of great interest as they often give the name of the village magnate, such as Tudda at Teddington, or the reason for their choice of site. The Thames itself, however, like all other important rivers vital to the topography, still bears the inherited Celtic name, thought to mean 'dark river', as does the Brent or Brigantia signifying a 'holy river' to which is added the Saxon suffix 'ford' at Brentford, indicating its importance for settlement. The suffix 'ey' as in Molesey (Mull's island) comes from the Anglo-Saxon 'ieg' or island and as with the eyots, or aits, on the Thames denotes land on a gravel terrace above the floods. The bends in the river, the Saxon 'hamms' where the water meadows folded and provided additional fertile alluvial deposits were particularly favoured by the farmers as at Petersham (Peohtric's ham[m]) and Twickenham (Twicca's ham[m]). Kingston, as its name implies, has special royal connections.

In the 7th century Surrey was under the king of Mercia, who founded Chertsey Abbey, which accumulated landholdings as far away as Petersham. When the Mercians were defeated by Egbert of Wessex about 829 the area known as Sudrie or Surrey in a charter of 722 was included in the kingdom of Wessex and Kingston, first heard of in 838, was the meeting place of a great council under King Egbert. During the 10th century West Saxon kings were crowned there until the Danish King Canute succeeded Edmund Ironside and ended the West Saxon dynasty.

The medieval kings began a process of royal control of the landscape between Hampton and Kew which is now vested in the Historic Royal Palaces Agency, the Crown Commissioners, the Royal Parks and the Royal Botanic Gardens. In 1197 Richard I gave up his royal prerogative over the river in return for a cash subvention. Ever since the Thames from Staines downstream has been under the control of the City of London. The City's Committee for the Thames and Canal Navigation was succeeded in 1857 by the Thames Conservancy, now part of the National Rivers Authority. The Port of London Authority assumed responsibility for the tidal Thames in 1908.

The royal palace at Shene, and later the palace at Hampton Court, were refuges for pleasure and from plague, with easy transport from Westminster. London was polluted and smoke-filled from the prevailing west winds. To escape the pollution William III, who suffered from asthma, abandoned Greenwich palace to the east of London and moved up-wind to Hampton Court as his out-of-town palace. There was always ready provision for the court at the Thames-side palaces. Not only were the fish plentiful but the royal larder could also be supplied with venison from the hunting grounds adjacent to the palaces.

The greatest amount of land under royal control was that reserved for hunting, which has had a vitally beneficial effect on the landscape of the area in terms of green space. Charles I was 'excessively affected to hunting' and found his father's old park at Richmond palace inadequate. In 1637 he made a new park up the hill of about 2,500 acres surrounded by eight miles of brick wall. It included the ancient Shene Chase and other royal manors, waste ground, commons and farms, ringed by Richmond, Kingston, Wimbledon, Putney and Mortlake. The central London royal parks, Greenwich and Hampton Court were all redesigned as formal or landscaped parks after the Restoration, but Richmond, having remained in the main a traditional natural deer park is now not only a remarkable green lung and recreational space for South London but a haven for wildlife.

The stretch of the Thames between Hampton and Kew, with its royal and noble patrons, is remarkable for the range and outstanding quality of its architecture – the Tudor and Wren palace of Hampton Court; the great castellated Syon House for Protector Somerset; the seventeenth-century Ham House, home of Charles II's most powerful minister; the gem of a Palladian villa at Marble Hill for George II's mistress; Horace Walpole's unique fantasy of Strawberry Hill; and the Princess Augusta's pagoda at Kew.

The effect of royal patronage on art and architecture is well appreciated, but the Crown's influence on landscape design is equally important. Throughout the seventeenth century the best garden designers were brought over from Europe: Salomon de

4. *Syon House* painted by Jan Griffier in the early eighteenth century (detail).
Reproduced by kind permission of the Duke of Northumberland

Caus to Richmond Palace by Renaissance Prince Henry, Mollet to Hampton Court by
Charles II and Daniel Marot for the later baroque layout there by William III. In
a reverse trend, after the eighteenth century our own English landscape gardening, patronised by the Crown and practised by Charles Bridgeman, William Kent,
'Capability' Brown and William Chambers, was emulated all over Europe.

5. *View from Richmond Hill* painted by
Peter Tillemans about 1730. Private collection

The concept of the Thames Palladian villa as a classical retreat emerged in the
second decade of the eighteenth century. Marble Hill had the advantage over
Chiswick of having the ideal situation advocated by Palladio for a villa, 'advantageous
and delicious as can be desired, being situated on a hillock of most easy ascent, at the
foot of which runs a navigable river'. It was this 'animated prospect' of the Thames,
with laden barges and colourful pleasure craft, which delighted riverside residents
from Hampton to Kew, particularly Horace Walpole at Strawberry Hill.

Soon after her accession Queen Victoria opened Hampton Court and Bushy Park
to the public and also Kew Gardens. Unlike Hampton Court, Kew Gardens, which
became the Royal Botanic Gardens, were not solely for pleasure but were to become a
scientific institution. Sir William Hooker, the first director, allowed the public in
every afternoon, but finally in 1916 the 'in for a penny' charge was initiated. Even
though charges have had to rise, Kew Gardens, as well as being pre-eminent for
research, is still one of the most popular London excursions.

Marble Hill, now in the care of English Heritage, unexpectedly came into public ownership in 1902 by an Act of Parliament following local opposition to the threatened development of the site. This was the first time that public concern had preserved a view as such. The original intention to save Marble Hill having been extended to the Surrey side of the Thames, thirty-nine acres of Petersham Meadows and a riverside promenade were vested in the Richmond Corporation after negotiation with the Dysart estates at Ham. Marble Hill and Thomson's Arcadian view from Richmond Hill were saved for posterity.

This area has attracted poets, painters, actors and musicians since at least the sixteenth century. Some of the most influential figures in the history of the Landscape Movement are associated with this part of the Thames; notably Alexander Pope, James Thomson, Horace Walpole and J.M.W. Turner. With the Thames as inspiration, the prospect and nature poetry, in the pastoral tradition, fused with gardening to create what is acknowledged as the country's greatest contribution to European culture: the naturalised landscaped garden.

Daniel Defoe, writing in his Tour in 1724, was the first to see the Thames as a collective landscape: 'There is a beauty of these things at a distance, taking them en passant, and in perspective, which few people value, and fewer understand'. Peter Tillemans *(plate 5)*, Jan Siberechts, Leonard Knyff *(plate 31)* and Antonio Joli all showed the beauties of such a representation of the Thames in their prospect views from Richmond Hill. In the mid-century two painters who lived in the locality, Augustin Heckel *(plate 30)* and Samuel Scott *(plate 26)*, painted detailed working scenes from the river bank, showing the diversity of the landscape, which will be seen in the descriptions of each area. Even in the eighteenth century the aristocratic world of wit and fashion accepted commercial neighbours who would not have been tolerated on country estates; there was a brick and tile manufactory in the Petersham meadows in close proximity to the much admired New Park garden, the stench of a tannery wafted into Pope's grotto and Walpole had some of his precious stained-glass windows blown out by a nearby gunpowder mill.

Richard Wilson sought out more Arcadian Claudian scenes of the Thames to paint at Marble Hill and Syon *(plate 40)*. J.M.W. Turner was also devoted to the Thames, having lived at Brentford, Isleworth and Twickenham at different times in his life and he painted many views of river scenes from Hampton to Kew. His Isleworth sketchbooks show an intimate knowledge of the working life of the river and its backwaters *(plate 1)*, but it is his idealised view of Thomson's 'matchless Vale of Thames' from Richmond Hill, which is his picturesque eulogy of the area *(plate 35)*. It is always the unifying Thames which is at the heart of artistic inspiration and the Frenchman who said to Alexander Pope at Twickenham: 'All this is very fine, but take away the river and it is good for nothing', did indeed speak with truth.

BUSHY PARK AND HURST PARK

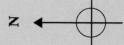

N

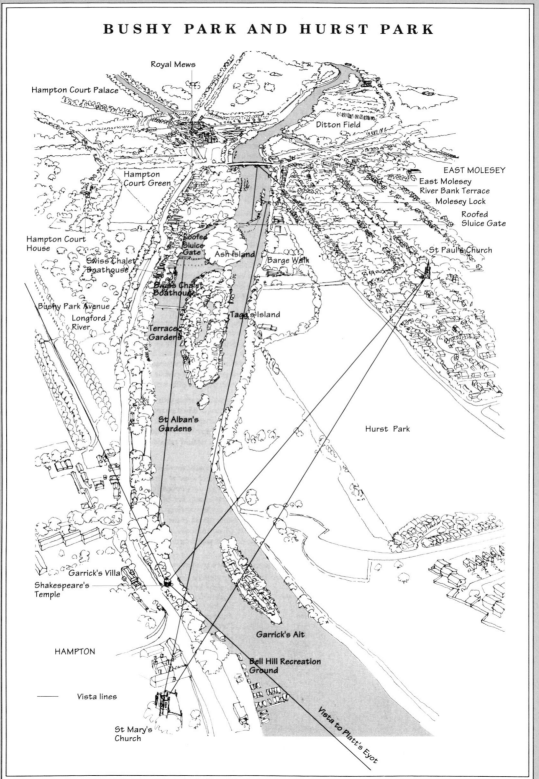

Royal Mews

Hampton Court Palace

Ditton Field

EAST MOLESEY

Hampton
Court Green

East Molesey
River Bank Terrace

Molesey Lock

Roofed
Sluice Gate

Hampton Court
House

Roofed
Sluice
Gate

Ash Island

Barge Walk

St Paul's Church

Swiss Chalet
Boathouse

Swiss Chalet
Boathouse

Bushy Park Avenue

Tagg's Island

Longford
River

Terrace
Gardens

St Alban's
Gardens

Hurst Park

Garrick's Villa

Shakespeare's
Temple

HAMPTON

Garrick's Ait

Bell Hill Recreation
Ground

——— Vista lines

St Mary's
Church

Vista to Platt's Eyot

BUSHY PARK AND HURST PARK

Landscape and natural history

The first reach between Hampton and Hampton Court bridge is characterised by open parkland running down to the water's edge, interspersed with boat-yards, houseboats and the waterfronts of Hampton and East Molesey.

The thick line of trees along the edge of Hampton water works and Platt's Eyot, the picturesque massing of the boat-yards and the old buildings of Hampton, rising up to the tower of St Mary's, contribute to the view which has been described as the gateway to the Greater London area. Beyond the enclosure of the trees, the corrugated iron boat sheds of Platt's Eyot and the wharves of Hampton, the reach opens to parkland. Bushy and Hurst Parks provide a broad expanse of open space on either side of the river, determining the main character of the reach. Hurst Park sweeps right down to the water's edge, while Bushy Park is set back behind a road and railings. The view from Platt's Eyot bridge, looking past the boat sheds in the foreground down to Shakespeare's Temple and Bushy Park beyond, shows the integration of working and formally designed landscapes which is characteristic of the entire stretch up to Kew.

Garrick's Villa and its riverside temple, dedicated to Shakespeare, provide the main visual focus of the reach, particularly when viewed against the backdrop of Hampton and St Mary's church. The classical lines of the temple contrast with the eccentric Edwardian exuberance of many of the houseboats and boathouses which line the reach, especially around Tagg's Island. The Edwardian feeling of the river still extends into the Barge Walk and Hurst Park itself, even though Tagg's Boathouse has recently been demolished and the race track is no longer in use.

Within Bushy Park the main avenues have been carefully maintained and replanted, but the extraordinary water garden and avenue landscape of Upper Lodge, within the park, are in urgent need of restoration. Bushy Park contains several woodland plantations and a large number of mature parkland trees, which add considerably to the appeal of the place for people and wildlife alike. The parkland trees, arranged in avenues, are mostly horse chestnuts and limes.

Although these trees do not support the exceptional diversity of invertebrates to be found in the ancient oaks and beeches of Richmond Park, they are of considerable value and provide homes for a similar range of cavity-nesting birds, including green woodpeckers, and also jackdaws and little owls which are rare in London. Mistletoe, now scarce in London, can be seen growing in several trees of various species.

Bushy Park contains some excellent wetland habitats, which are host to a number of locally and nationally rare plants, as well as to a variety of fish and aquatic invertebrates. Very inconspicuous as a plant, and previously thought to be extinct in Middlesex, mudwort was discovered in a marshy area by local botanists in 1986. Bushy Park has a series of canals, ponds and avenues surrounded by dry acidic grassland and bracken. The grasslands support an abundant invertebrate fauna, including butterflies such as small copper, small heath and meadow brown, large numbers of grasshoppers and a good variety of moths. Bracken has taken over sizeable areas of the park, replacing the diverse acid grasslands with a virtual monoculture. Being unpalatable or even poisonous to most animals, bracken is not controlled by grazing.

The busy Hampton Court Road runs along the Middlesex bank, separating Bushy Park from the river. St Albans Gardens weave between the road and river, a narrow public park of mown grass with mature plane and horse chestnut trees. The river here is non-tidal and the trees reflect in the still water. On the river's edge, below the level of the busy road, the constant flow of traffic is less intrusive, allowing a sense of the peace of the water and parkland. Remnants of earlier riverside gardens can be traced in occasional crumbling steps and planters. The Longford river provides a valuable connecting link between Bushy Park and the Thames, with a small marshy area at its mouth. The outflow from the Longford river, although becoming clogged by brambles and chestnut seedlings, creates an attractive tributary of gravel beaches, flag irises and nesting birds. The waterfront park is interrupted before Hampton Court Green by a run of inter-war houses and three-storey flat-roofed apartment buildings.

The Surrey bank is more open. Except where trees have sprouted up into a barrier between the towpath and the river, the close-mown grass of Hurst Park runs down to the river's edge and the open space extends back to Hurst Road. The towpath and gravel beaches are heavily used by wildfowl and people alike, with access both from East Molesey along the river and from the car park. The cars are kept back from the river's edge and partially screened behind trees and earth bunds. The incursions of 1960s housing into the park, including a particularly dominating block of flats, and modern office and residential buildings into the Barge Walk, have detracted from the sense of space. The linear fence division, between Hurst Park and the former racecourse land, leaves the area feeling rather unresolved. The land will be managed as a single unit when the whole park comes under the ownership of the Borough of Elmbridge. But the basic openness survives, backed by a thick massing of garden trees pierced only by the spire of St Paul's church.

Contrasting with the scale of the open spaces, Tagg's Island and Garrick's Ait are covered by single-storey bungalows; an unexpected note of busy domesticity. The bungalows are largely made of wood and painted bright colours. A variety of jetties and boats cluster at the foot of individual and manicured small gardens. The few trees between the houses help to reduce the impact of the buildings in the middle of the river corridor. Garrick's Ait has a small wild area, on the downstream end, where a large willow hangs over the water, providing a good duck nesting ground. Tagg's Island, despite development for residential use, is a valuable nesting haven for waterfowl with its internal lagoon, connected to the river. Carp use the sheltered water as a breeding ground. The edges have been planted with yellow flag, great hairy willow-herb and ornamental trees such as weeping willow. The island's human residents, living in modern houseboats resembling bungalows placed on rafts moored around the edge of the lagoon, share their home with up to twenty pairs of Canada geese and lesser numbers of mute swans, coots and great crested grebes. Off the upstream tip of Tagg's Island lies a tiny island with three weeping willows. The National Rivers Authority has enhanced the island and set it aside for nesting wildfowl. This and the Hurst Park bank are also heavily used by the Hampton flock of swans. The island, being trampled by waterfowl and used for mooring boats, has no vegetation apart from the willows.

Ash Island has a far more natural appearance than the other islands in this reach. The island is covered in woodland and the western half has sycamore, weeping willow, elm, and hawthorn with a dense ground flora of nettles, rose-bay willow-herb, ivy and bramble. The trees on the eastern end of the island are sparser and there is little cover. The island, though of quite a wild appearance, does receive a fair degree of disturbance due to the numerous houseboats moored along its banks. Dogs and cats are ever present but mallards manage to nest.

Opposite Ash Island on the Surrey side, next to the Barge Walk, there is a well-vegetated stony bank and a green edge to the path. The bank is well used by Canada geese, mallard and coot. The land between East Molesey Cricket Club and Hampton Court bridge has some trees and an area rapidly colonising with wild plants, though the site is now subject to various planning permissions.

Molesey Lock forms a discrete sub-area, dominated by the architecture of the lock, the roofed sluice gates, Lutyens's bridge and the Edwardian housing terrace which runs along the East Molesey river bank. The river scene remains much as Sisley painted it in 1874 *(plate 6)*, bustling with boating activity. The sub-area has a feeling of enclosure, contained by the lock and weir walls, by the thick trees covering Ash Island and the banks of spacious gardens, by the East Molesey terrace, and by the powerful brick and stone bridge. High chainlink fencing on the river's edge beneath the Royal Mews and the large fibreglass motor cruisers, parked three deep, are incongruous elements in the scene. The river along the edge of the Royal Mews's garden has a high stone bank and a good deal of secluded scrub of value to wildlife, hosting woodpeckers, jays and other woodland birds.

The Terrace Gardens is one of the few places where the river's banks are not constructed of artificial material. The water margin sports clumps of yellow flag, reed sweet-grass, small patches of water mint, and one or two plants of great water dock, a species uncommon in London. The leaves of great water dock are enormous green blades up to a metre long, making it most distinctive on the water's edge.

Historical background
As a small rural village Hampton's staples were boat building and farming; there was a windmill on Hampton Hill for grinding corn between 1785 and 1876. By 1831 however, the village was growing and old St Mary's church was rebuilt for the

expanding population. Suburban development followed the course of the Thames Valley railway, opened in 1864 with an inevitable impact on river traffic. In the last quarter of the nineteenth century an area of terraced housing was developed and christened New Hampton (later known as Hampton Hill), and Hampton began to merge into Teddington round the back of the royal park. A major expansion took place in the 1970s when over 1,700 houses were built on the market gardens and nurseries to the north west of the village.

After the 1852 Metropolis Water Act three companies moved their intakes upriver to Hampton. The works were built in a row along the Staines road around 1855 to Italianate designs by Joseph Quick, engineer to the Southwark and Vauxhall Company. The later building of the Southwark and Vauxhall at Riverdale (1899-1901) has all the appearance of an oversize but still elegant French Empire orangery.

Platt's Eyot was the base of Immisch and Company, set up in 1899 to produce electric-powered launches, with a sequence of charging stations installed up and down the Thames. Only the steam-driven generating station on the island remains of this ambitious venture, ruined by the advent of petrol-driven combustion engines. The island then became the base from 1914 to 1960 for the Thorneycroft boatyard, building motor torpedo boats for the Royal Navy through both world wars. The raised level at the upper end of the island is due to spoil tipped from the reservoir excavations at Hampton.

The actor David Garrick bought Hampton House in 1754 and transformed it, with major alterations by Robert Adam, into a classical villa (see *pages 31-36*). Garrick's Temple dedicated to Shakespeare still stands in a garden owned by the London Borough of Richmond. A large house was built in Garrick's riverside garden in 1923, but it was generally much disliked for its impact on the landscape, and it was eventually purchased by Hampton Urban District Council and demolished in 1932. The public open space covers only part of Garrick's original riverside garden, which has been split in two by a high wooden fence. It misses the serpentine paths and the weeping willow as well as the cypresses planted by Walpole.

Much of Bushy Park was first enclosed in the early sixteenth century. Miles of 1530s park wall still survive and the oak pollards on the park's north-west boundary were probably planted in 1536. Henry VIII appears to have been responsible for the great stands of oak recorded in the seventeenth century and felled by the Duke of Clarence at the beginning of the nineteenth century. The great north and west avenues were first laid out by the fashionable gardeners London and Wise between 1689 and 1699. The Chestnut Avenue, with its unprecedented quadrupled grandeur, was intended as a state approach to a new north front by Christopher Wren. This great scheme was forestalled by William's death.

More modestly, Garrick aligned his temple on the Hampton avenue, which was replanted in the 1950s. As a result of a land exchange for tramway access along Hampton Court Road in the 1860s, a small portion of Garrick's garden – the north-east corner containing an informal mount – was transferred into the Stockyard lands in Bushy Park. The mount still survives, now much warrened by rabbits. A large part of the rest of the garden has been developed for housing, but the mount will be conserved by the Royal Parks.

The canal through Bushy Park, known as the Longford river, was dug in 1639 from a tributary of the river Colne to supply water for the household and gardens at Hampton Court. It was also made use of by the Earl of Halifax, ranger of Bushy Park under William III, who diverted water into the water gardens round Upper Lodge. These water gardens were much admired by the landscape gardener Stephen Switzer. Some of the earthworks remain and there are hopes of restoring them.

Bushy Park and Hampton Court were both opened to the public by Queen Victoria in 1838, becoming a much-loved local amenity. During the Second World War an American air force base and the Supreme Headquarters of the Allied Expeditionary Forces were located in Bushy Park. Following the war there was political pressure to turn the base into local housing. Fortunately this was rejected and in 1963 the base was finally demolished and the land returned to park.

Hampton Court House on Hampton Green was built in 1757 by the 2nd Earl of Halifax for his mistress Anne Maria Donaldson. The garden was centred on a lake adapted from a gravel pit, but its great feature was a grotto designed by Thomas Wright, the wizard of Durham, adorned with astronomical motifs and dedicated to Venus. The grotto was restored by Diana Reynell and Simon Verity in 1983-86 and can be visited by appointment.

Hurst Park originated as Molesey Hurst, a common meadow belonging to the manor of Molesey Matham, but in the early eighteenth century its transformation began into one of the great people's playgrounds of London. Archery, cricket, boxing, cock-fighting, golf and horse-racing – all found a place here; it was also a favoured rendezvous for duellists. In the early nineteenth century the Hurst rose to fame

for its bare-knuckle fights, with crowds of up to 10,000 arriving by road and river, until the sport was outlawed in a ruling at Kingston Assizes in 1824. But the attraction of 'Hampton Races', fostered by the Duke of Clarence (later William IV) meant that the Hurst continued in popular importance. The annual 'Cockney Derby' held in June was a great London holiday which Dickens described in terms of 'picturesque poverty' in *Nicholas Nickleby*. The derbies ended in 1887 when the Jockey Club refused to renew the course licence on the grounds of its lack of proper maintenance.

In 1899 a new course, called Hurst Park, was opened, surrounded by a wooden fence seven feet high. The visual intrusiveness of this huge fence running within a few feet of the Thames provoked numerous protests, but to no avail – the owners threatened to sell the land for building if they were balked. From 1891 to 1962 Hurst Park was one of the most successful racecourses in the country. In 1962, although the course was still running at a profit, the owners decided to sell the site for housing and at the subsequent auction even the turf, well known for its springiness, was sold. The wide strip of grassland which comprises Hurst Park today was preserved in the terms of the planning permission for the housing put up in the early 1960s.

The picturesque shanties and bungalows on Garrick's Ait date from the 1920s, when the island, which for centuries had been covered with willows and osiers used for the local basket industry, was broken into small plots and sold off for development.

Tagg's Island has had a more colourful history. Originally Crown land belonging to the honour of Hampton Court, it had for centuries been squatted by families who made a living from basket-making. It was bought in about 1850 by a property speculator named Francis Kent who evicted the squatters. Thomas Tagg, of the famous Tagg family of watermen and boat-builders, moved his boat-building business on to part of the island in the 1850s and soon acquired the lease of the whole, In 1873 he built a hotel on the island which became a fashionable resort, custom being attracted in part by his reputation as a boat-builder to high society.

In 1912 the lease was taken over by Fred Karno, who had one of the grandiose houseboats moored alongside. He transformed the island, lavishing thousands on a re-built hotel, the 'Karsino', and spectacular gardens. Guests and their cars were ferried over in 'large and artistic punts', and the pleasures included tennis, croquet, bowls, boating, and of course musical comedy shows put on in the enormous 800-seat Palm Court. The Karsino opened in 1913 and for several years it was a glorious pleasure palace. But changing tastes and the demise of the music hall saw its fortunes decline.

In 1926 Karno sold the tenancy rights before being declared bankrupt the following year. Over the next few years Tagg's Island was regularly recast – as 'a miniature Palm Beach' or the new 'Thames Riviera' – by a succession of ever-optimistic new operators. The hotel was finally demolished in 1971, but plans for a new hotel or block of flats or sports centre have never materialised, and it has reverted to

something of its semi-rural appearance of the days before Tagg.

On the Middlesex bank opposite Tagg's Island, the Swiss Chalet was originally brought over from Switzerland in about 1882 as a garden feature for a now demolished house called Riverholme a few yards downstream. Its theatricality seems of a piece with the history of this stretch of the river.

The river has always been a highway for the movement of goods in and out of the capital, and by the nineteenth century barges hauled by 50 men or a dozen horses were carrying up to 200 tons of material. But as the traffic increased, the *ad hoc* arrangement of wooden weirs and dams, which created sufficient depth of water for navigation in the upper reaches, became increasingly unsatisfactory. The lock at East Molesey was opened in 1815 as the last part of a series to improve the upper Thames navigation (locks were also built at Chertsey, Shepperton, Sunbury and Teddington), and it has frequently been modernised since then.

Apart from commercial traffic, at weekends and holidays the lock was crowded with pleasure boats. Jerome K. Jerome thought Molesey the busiest lock on the river and in 1889 described how, 'I have stood and watched it sometimes, when you could not see any water at all, but only a brilliant tangle of bright blazers, and gay caps, and saucy hats, and many-coloured parasols, and silken rugs, and cloaks and streaming ribbons, and dainty whites'. Molesey still retains some of the atmosphere of Victorian and Edwardian holidays.

6. Alfred Sisley: *Regatta at Molesey* (1874). Musée d'Orsay, Paris

HAMPTON COURT

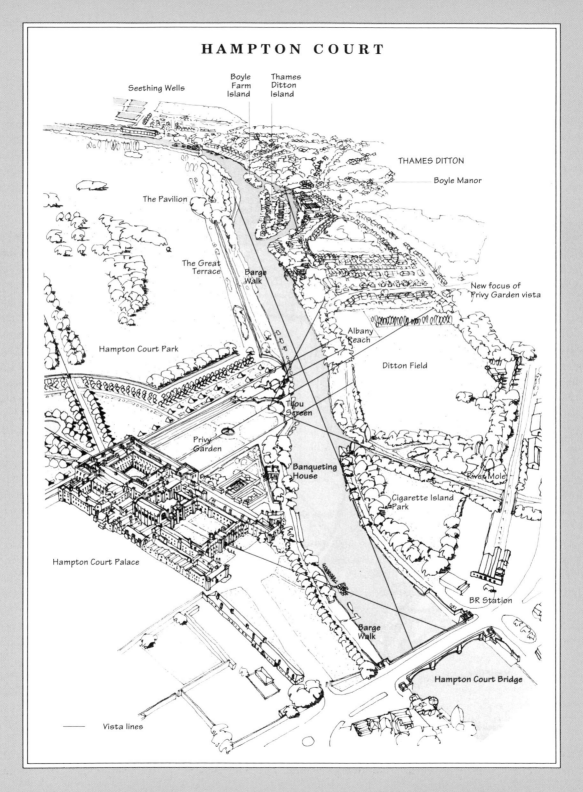

Seething Wells

Boyle
Farm
Island

Thames
Ditton
Island

THAMES DITTON

Boyle Manor

The Pavilion

The Great
Terrace

Barge
Walk

New focus of
Privy Garden vista

Albany
Reach

Hampton Court Park

Ditton Field

Tijou
Screen

Privy
Garden

Banqueting
House

River Mole

Cigarette Island
Park

Hampton Court Palace

BR Station

Barge
Walk

Hampton Court Bridge

—— Vista lines

2

N

HAMPTON COURT

Landscape and natural history

The reach from Hampton Court bridge to Seething Wells is dominated by Hampton Court palace. The verticals of the warm, red brick of the turrets and chimneys and the horizontals of the lead and tile roofs combine to create one of the most unusual skylines in London. The Palace Barge Walk, as it curves around the bend of the river, brings a stately sweep of rural open space, backed by Hampton Court Park. The palace and its baroque setting remain remarkably untroubled by the growth of the surrounding city with much of the developments on the Surrey bank softened by garden trees. Long views of the Surrey hills beyond can still be glimpsed.

Viewed from Hampton Court bridge, the Wolsey frontage of the palace is at its most spectacular, with the towers and chimneys rising behind the gatehouse and reflected in the river. However, concrete block bank retentions and the paraphernalia of tourist boat businesses detract from the visual impact and the whole view of the palace is gradually being obscured by a line of boundary sycamores. The Banqueting House, poised on the edge of the Barge Walk and river, is also becoming hidden. The graceful arches of the brick and stone Hampton Court bridge by Lutyens stand out as a clear terminus to the reach.

The view of the Wren façade through the Tijou screen and the Privy Garden has recently been revealed for the first time in two centuries (see *pages 37-43*). Unfor-

tunately this view is similarly marred by concrete structures and tourist moorings. In fact the whole Barge Walk around Hampton Court Park fails to do justice to the setting. Sporadic ornamental purple cherries and pink hawthorns detract from the Pavilion Terrace and complement neither the scale nor the grandeur of the palace; nor do they contribute to the wildlife value of the grassland. By contrast a fine old stone pine in the Pavilion grounds and mature cedars in Thames Ditton stand out as landmarks along the river. The Barge Walk river bank has an interesting range of plants, some preferring wet situations and some the drier bank top, but all thriving in the open, unshaded conditions of this stretch of the river bank. The very narrow strip of unmown grass along both sides of the towpath contains a surprisingly rich flora including agrimony, hardheads and meadow sweet. A number of plants rare in London are also found here – wild clary, vervain, meadow cranesbill and many others. By extending meadow management, much of the grassland along the Barge Walk could be equally rich.

The Barge Walk trees take three forms: a self-sown woodland against the park wall, planted hawthorns and cherries in the grassland, and alder and other trees growing at the water's edge. A management plan for this important area would maintain the woodland strip without losing the valuable views into the park or damaging the wall and grassland. The river edge

would be improved by coppicing the alder and willow trees.

The bank protections on the Surrey side are in worse condition. Whole concrete panels and metal grills are collapsing into the water. The avenue of mature chestnuts along the southern side of the Cigarette Island towpath screens the railway and creates a strong edge to the river, while still leaving the path open to the water. Interplantings of evergreen oak, either side of the towpath will gradually block walkers' views. The Mole and Ember tributary separates Cigarette Island from Ditton Field. Its wilder banks create an interesting contrast with the trim edges of the Thames and frame the channel to the railway bridge with longer grass and willows. Cormorants and herons can be seen fishing here and it might be possible to create a marshy habitat by regrading the river edge in places.

Ditton Field is given over to formal recreation pitches and sports pavilions. Chain-link fencing, an all-weather hockey pitch and a strong line of boundary lombardy poplars no longer provide the pastoral vista of water meadows from the palace, but at least the open space and trees leave the view open to the Surrey hills beyond. This particular vista now forms the focal terminus of the Privy Garden and needs to be considered with care.

The group of trees at the southern end of Ditton Field separates the open spaces

7. Hampton Court bridge from Molesey Lock. Photograph by Lucilla Phelps

from the built. Thereafter the Surrey bank becomes industrial and residential. Brick factory buildings and boat clubs scale down to dense single-storey bungalow plots on Thames Ditton Island and its side-channel. The fine nineteenth-century factory buildings and iron bridge, eighteenth-century Boyle Manor (now the Home of Compassion) and the seventeenth-century inn create an interesting historic waterfront for Thames Ditton, surrounded by colourful bungalows lining the narrow side-channel.

The trees on tiny Boyle Farm Island and the southern end of Thames Ditton Island combine with trees in large private gardens beyond Boyle Manor to create an impression of rural peace before the tree-less terraces of 1960s and 1970s housing and three-storey apartments further downstream.

Historical background

In 1514 Cardinal Wolsey leased about a thousand acres of land in the beautiful bend of the Thames at Hampton from the knights hospitallers of the Order of St John of Jerusalem. The knights had established there, on land granted by the Crown in 1312, an agricultural estate for raising funds for the order's priory at Clerkenwell. Henry VII first enclosed an area called 'Hampton Parke' when he was using the hospitallers' *camera* as an outstation for Richmond Palace. Wolsey extended the area, emparking demesne arable land, a process of accretion that was continued by Henry VIII and James I. Vestiges of ridge and furrow in both Bushy Park and Home Park bear witness to the parkland's medieval use for arable farming. The central area of Bushy Park contains what

has been claimed to be the best preserved medieval field system in Middlesex.

Wolsey gave his ostentatious palace to Henry in 1525 in a vain effort to save his fall, but in 1529 his goods were seized and he was arrested for treason. He died in the next year. It has been deduced that the palace's puzzling location – away from the Hampton village and thus not on the manor house site – derives from its being on the site of the hospitallers' *camera*, which was located here in order to be close to their sheep walk. After Wolsey's death, Henry began further work on the palace, spending more and more time there. Henry's passion for hunting led him to develop the park and some of the seventeenth-century vistas followed the lines of his straight rides.

The interleaved gravel and sand in this vicinity provided building materials throughout Hampton Court's history, as did the local clay for the bricks. Henry VIII had bricks made on site, as well as at Kingston, Hampton and Hampton Wick and further afield. An engraving of 1736 shows what appear to be smoking brick kilns or clamps to the west of the palace, apparently on Hampton Green. What had been thought to be a moat north of the Privy Garden seems to have been a gravel pit in Wolsey's time, and Knyff's bird's eye view of Hampton Court in 1702 shows a gravel pit on Hampton Green *(plate 12)*.

The earliest gardens at Hampton Court were laid out in the area between the palace and the river, first for Wolsey and then for Henry. In 1690-91 William III remodelled Charles II's simple parterre in the Privy Garden. (The story of the Privy Garden and its restoration is given on *pages 37-43*). Hampton Court was essentially a joint enterprise between William and Mary and when Mary died of smallpox in 1694, William was too dispirited to continue the building and gardening projects. Only the fire which four years later destroyed Whitehall Palace forced him to proceed with the plans for Hampton Court in order to receive the Court.

William demolished the Water Gallery and in 1701 extended the garden to the Barge Walk, where Jean Tijou's wrought-iron screens (originally intended for the Great Fountain Garden) were erected. With the recent decision to restore the Privy Garden and the clearance of the site, one can now look back from the Barge Walk through the Tijou screens to Wren's façade and see the whole ensemble.

The castellated Banqueting House, containing some of Grinling Gibbons's carvings from the demolished Water Gallery, was built on a raised terrace overlooking the Thames and the compartmented gardens, made from the Tudor pondyards, where Queen Mary had indulged her passion for florists' flowers and exotic botanical collections in new 'glass cases'. The Banqueting House above the Barge Walk is a delightfully evocative Thames-side garden building. William, who died in 1702, also had the Great Terrace along the Thames made, extending half a mile from the end of the Broad Walk to an oval bowling green around which Wren built four pavilions, one of which survives. This was designed, unlike the earlier straight rides and avenues, for the enjoyment of the panorama of the Thames landscape beyond the park and Stephen Switzer admired it as 'the noblest work of that kind in Europe'.

Hampton Court is a royal landscape without equal, but on the Surrey side the Thames is a landscape of popular pleasure. Despite its unpicturesque name, Cigarette Island – the tail of land at the confluence of the Ember, Mole and Thames – was much admired for its picturesque qualities and the view of the palace from here was a favourite among artists. However at the turn of the century, the view was obscured first by the houseboats which up until 1931 lined the Surrey bank at this point – Cigarette Island used to be called Davis's Ait and was renamed after a particularly grand boat moored here – and second by the mass of weekend holiday homes made from wood and corrugated iron, converted railway carriages, buses and caravans, known ironically as Venice on Thames. In the early twentieth century, the holiday homes covered the island and adjacent meadows. The final solution to what was felt to be an eyesore was found when the

Office of Works bought the island in 1935 and turned it into a public park. This was done with the express aim of preserving the view from and of Hampton Court.

There appears to have been a ferry on the site of Hampton Court bridge from at least Tudor times. The ferry was first replaced in 1753 by a bridge in chinoiserie style, which had successors in wood and iron. The present brick and ferro-concrete structure, designed by the Surrey county engineer W.P. Robinson in collaboration with Lutyens, was opened in 1933.

In the eighteenth century Thames Ditton had a small coterie of fashionable houses with the grounds of Ditton House and Boyle Farm sharing the river frontage below Ditton Island. In 1911 the *Victoria County History* noted that the latter estate was 'gradually being cut up' and that Ditton House's 'beautiful sweeping lawns once famous for their smoothness are now only a rough field'. However, in the late eighteenth and early nineteenth centuries Boyle Farm rivalled Strawberry Hill as a fashionable centre for society. Its famous Dandies' Fête of 1827 reputedly cost £2,500 to stage. In 1787 Walpole remarked that Miss Boyle, who carved sculptures for a chimney piece and painted panels for the library, had 'real genius'. The garden, with its cedars, would have commanded fine views across Thames Ditton Island to Hampton Court, as the island remained undeveloped until the early part of this century.

Thames Ditton Ferry Works of 1879 - 88 boasted the earliest known example of a saw-tooth northern light. Symbolically, the works were taken over in 1911 for the manufacture of cars. The works have now been restored and sub-divided for other uses.

3

PORTSMOUTH ROAD

N

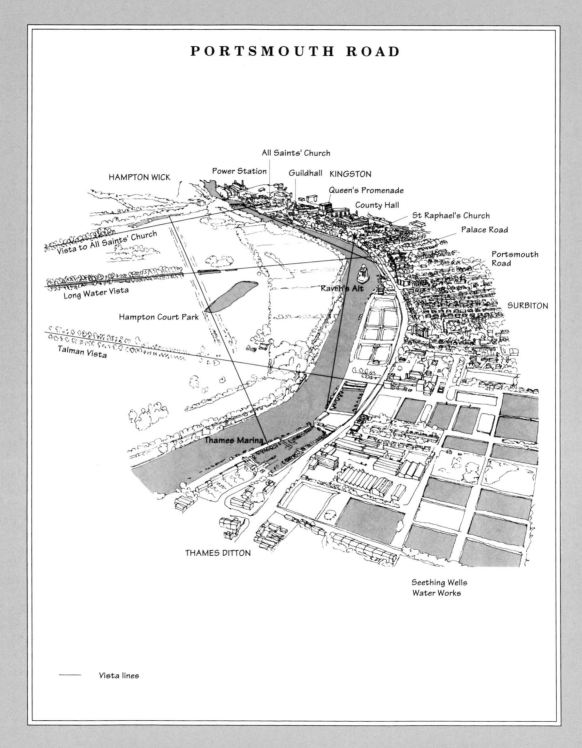

All Saints' Church

HAMPTON WICK

Power Station

Guildhall

KINGSTON

Queen's Promenade

County Hall

St Raphael's Church

Palace Road

Vista to All Saints' Church

Portsmouth Road

Long Water Vista

Raven's Ait

SURBITON

Hampton Court Park

Talman Vista

Thames Marina

THAMES DITTON

Seething Wells
Water Works

—— Vista lines

PORTSMOUTH ROAD

Landscape and natural history

The Portsmouth Road reach runs north from Seething Wells up to Kingston. The reach has a character of wide open grassland, interrupted only by trees, park and water works' walls and the Portsmouth Road block of flats. Hampton Court Park extends over the entire Middlesex side right up to Hampton Wick, while the Surrey bank divides between the water works and the Queen's Promenade.

The Portsmouth Road follows the river the length of the reach on the Surrey side. This is one of the only sections of the upstream London Thames where a road has been built alongside the river. The busy road and associated linear developments make a harsh contrast with the rhythm of parkland and historic town waterfronts which characterise the rest of the river.

Hampton Court Park is held in the circling sweep of the Thames, as its flow curves from south to north. Charles II's Long Water and baroque avenues still radiate across the park, aligning on points over the river in Kingston and Surbiton. Planting along the river banks lifts the eye to distant views of the tree-covered Surrey Hills on the skyline, broken only by a series of church spires. From much of the park one has the impression of a continuing seventeenth-century landscape, where deer still graze the wild grass between long avenues of lime trees. At points where flat-roofed blocks of apartments and offices intrude into the scene from Hampton Wick

and across the river, the impact is therefore particularly jarring.

A band of riverside trees softens the impact of the Surrey bank developments on the park by blocking the ground level view. Of the three main *patte d'oie* avenues, the Kingston All Saints' church vista still remains intact; the Long Water vista now focuses on an uncomfortable assortment of three to six storey apartment blocks; and the Talman vista terminates in the recently listed Seething Wells pumping station. The north-south cross avenue would focus on the Thames Marina development, but at present the vista terminates in trees at either end. A programme of replanting the Hampton Court avenues is well underway. The Hampton Court Park stud farm works within the existing planting structure, but the fairways, greens and bunkers of the golf course strike an incongruous note in the grazed grassland.

Like Bushy Park, Hampton Court Park lies on the river terrace gravels and contains extensive acid grassland and a variety of ponds and canals. It has far fewer trees than Bushy Park, and these are mostly in the lime avenues. The golf course fairways in the southern half of the park are kept close mown, but the roughs contain an excellent acidic grassland flora. The northern half is grazed by sheep as well as deer, so the turf tends to be rather shorter than in Bushy Park and bracken invasion is not a problem.

The area of greatest nature conservation

interest lies along the south-eastern edge of the golf course, alongside the Thames towpath near Jubilee Gate. The number of rare plants here include subterranean clover, which forms large drifts of white flowers in May. The many anthills in the area, and indeed all over the park, are topped with the rare changing forget-me-not. Pride of place among the plants of Hampton Court Park, however, must go to autumn squill. During August and September, hundreds of these beautiful lilies send up their spikes of purple flowers along the south-eastern edge of the park; this is the only sizeable population in south-east England.

The Barge Walk continues along the length of the Middlesex bank, providing a peaceful, uninterrupted, riverside path of 4.5 kilometres from Kingston bridge to Hampton Court bridge. The trees which back the walk give a sense of scale and enclosure in the expansive landscape, but the suckering of diseased elms and rampant poplars have created a dense and ragged barrier which blocks off any glimpses into the park. The proliferation of young growth would need cyclical cutting to create a mosaic pattern of open, dense regrowth and woodland areas, of particular benefit to birds and woodland flora. Where ornamental cherries have been planted and scrub has established between the walk and the water's edge, the traditional relationship between the towing path and the river is destroyed. The low vegetated banks and the gravel path work well with the context, but the sparse municipal benches might be improved. The fine mature plane trees by the Lodge and Park Field help to blend the buildings into the landscape, but the concrete fencing panels beyond and the white railings of the Coach House detract from the rural character of the Barge Walk.

Behind the park wall and indeed walled off from the rest of the park, are the Hampton Court paddocks. Lying on alluvial deposits from the Thames, the grasslands here are of a very different character to those of the rest of the park, being much damper and of neutral pH. The greatest botanical importance of the fields is the marshy vegetation associated with a series of ditches which criss-cross them. There is a wonderful diversity of wetland plants with numerous London rarities, including water speedwell and marsh arrow-grass. The northernmost three or four fields are cut for hay, while several others are grazed by sheep, by the queen's horses and the Prince of Wales's polo ponies, as well as by an abundance of rabbits. This sympathetic management has helped to form an area with one of the largest numbers of naturalised wetland plants to be found in such a small space almost anywhere in London.

Across the Thames, the Seething Wells water works provide a substantial area of open space, linking down to the river and separating Thames Ditton from Surbiton; a welcome relief from the continuous built-up swathe along the Surrey bank from Kingston through Surbiton and Thames Ditton to East Molesey. The water works are now largely obsolete and Seething Wells presents the largest area (seven hectares between the road and the river) under consideration for redevelopment along the whole of the upstream river.

The river frontage is formed by high Victorian banks of arched brick walls, topped by broom and willow. The electric yellow of flowering broom is dramatic against the dark purple of the bricks. The sunken honeycomb of empty settling basins and filter beds has an impressive scale of Victorian engineering. Together with the gothic effect of the castellated pumping stations and the substantial iron railings along either side of the road, the water works have created an open area of bold, functional spaces in an otherwise unremitting density of inter-war suburban housing. In places where the basins have been re-used as a marina, the form and character of the area is retained and the use, while updated, still relates to the river. An area of offices and showrooms behind the marina and the introduction of car parking at eye-level between the road and the river relate less well to the water.

The reservoirs, which were built on the site of a spring, have steep brick banks, draped in ivy-leaved toadflax, ivy, and stonecrop and are encrusted with mosses and lichens. The internal grass banks are three metres deep and have great richness of plant species. The secret of these steep grassland meadows is that for nearly 150 years, since construction, no fertilisers or pesticides have been used for fear of contaminating the drinking water. The grassy slopes appear to be composed largely of a dry, calcareous substrate with old brick and stonework, the cracks of which have been colonised by plants. The calcareous base means that alkaline-loving plants have flourished although the floristic picture is complicated by areas of more acidic substrate and the differing aspects of the banks. Liberally scattered throughout the meadows are wildflowers such as burnet saxifrage, common St John's wort,

hoary plantain, salad burnet, and, unusually, three types of scabious: devil's bit, field, and the rarer small scabious, which together form mauve drifts, alive with bees and butterflies.

The grassland has been kept largely free of scrub, although there are some bushes: dog rose, elder, and birch are scattered here and there, but it is broom which is the most abundant, particularly along the top of the river wall. It is beneath the broom that the Canada geese make their large, down-lined nests. Other birds, such as great crested grebes, are found in the reservoirs in the breeding season, but the small size of the water bodies and the scarcity of any food in the water limits the bird population.

A short stretch of boat clubs and a pub separate the water works from the Queen's Promenade. The bright white paint and large signs of the restaurant, echoed on Raven's Ait, stand out prominently on the river bend. Beyond the bend, the Queen's Promenade retains much of its Victorian character with colourful flowerbeds, shrubberies, strips of lawn and cast iron railings. The long narrow space down beside the water is very popular with young and old alike. Trees, shrubs and the change in level help to reduce the impact of cars on the Portsmouth Road. However, many of the trees are now in poor condition and the access points from the road pavement to the Promenade have become obscured.

Large Victorian houses on the eastern side of the Portsmouth Road have gradually been replaced by blocks of apartments. Some of the blocks are up to eight storeys high, dwarfing the surrounding houses and standing out for miles around. 'Thames Haven' and 'Anglers Reach' are particularly intrusive, dominating the bend in the river between Seething Wells and the Queen's Promenade.

Historical background

Surbiton, although not mentioned in Domesday, existed as a farming hamlet from as early as the twelfth century. But by the early 1700s its seclusion and closeness to town brought it a new role, as a 'Private Place, long mark'd to entertain / Kept Mistresses e'er since great William's Reign'. It never had the cachet of the lower river, and a spa at Seething Wells appears to have failed fairly swiftly.

The earliest house in Surbiton seems to have been Berrylands Farm on Surbiton Hill, but by the early nineteenth century a number of villas such as Surbiton House and Surbiton Lodge had been built around the hamlet, and maps show them in extensive landscaped grounds. However, with the arrival of the London and South Western Railway in 1836 after the councillors of Kingston declined a station in the town, modern Surbiton, or Kingston-on-Railway as it was then known, was born. The 1808 Enclosure Act enabled the common and farm land to be comprehensively parcelled up for development, and this proceeded apace after the opening of the station in 1838. After the Surbiton Improvement Act of 1855, development was overseen and controlled by the Surbiton Improvement Commissioners. This led to a high quality of development, much of which survives, and helped to give Surbiton the title 'Queen of the Suburbs', a name later appropriated by Ealing.

The purer waters of the upper Thames also attracted some of the works supplying water to the expanding Victorian metropolis. Up river from Raven's Ait, on the site of the Seething Wells spa, the Lambeth Waterworks Company opened in 1852 and the Chelsea Waterworks in 1856. The steam-powered machinery has gone, but most of the buildings remain as monuments to high Victorian engineering. The Chelsea Company's Norman towers designed by James Simpson in 1852 are now listed.

While the contrast between the suburban and industrial Surrey side and the rural and emparked Middlesex side seems complete here, Palace Road was nicely aligned on the main vista in the Hampton Court Park along the Long Water, and the roadside planting of limes nods to the great avenue across the river.

Queen's Promenade was given its royal name in 1856, opened unwittingly by Queen Victoria after a well-placed diversion forced her to drive along the adjoining road on return from one of her visits to Claremont. She was not pleased when she learnt of the ruse. The road had been newly improved, having long been a hazard where it bent sharply with the line of the river. The burghers of Kingston had rejected as too costly a scheme by Brunel to straighten the river. The course was eventually modified in 1852-54, using spoil from the excavations at Seething Wells.

The promenade was first conceived by the property developer William Woods, with the intention of providing an exclusive walk between Raven's Ait and St Raphael's church for the residents of his new villas on the Portsmouth Road. But in return for assistance with its construction, Woods agreed to the walk being made into a public promenade and eventually, in 1896, it was extended all the way to Kingston.

On the Middlesex side, a band of meadowland separated the Hampton Court Park from the Barge Walk and the river. Rocque's plan of 1754 shows how the cross avenue joining the ends of the great avenues shut out this aspect of the river, except for the vistas themselves and the Lower Wilderness, added during William and Mary's reign.

The Home or House Park is dominated by the goose foot of avenues. This originated with the great canal planted with 'sweete rows of lime trees', designed by André and Gabriel Mollet for Charles II in the French Grand Manner. The two outer avenues were planted later for William and Mary, resulting in the famous *patte d'oie,* which complemented the new east front aligned by Wren on the Mollet canal. The three avenues radiate from the semicircular Great Fountain Garden in front of the palace, for which Daniel Marot designed the elaborate parterre shown in his proposals sketch of 1689. The overgrown yews are being left here, unlike those in the Privy Garden, and the lime arcade has been restored.

Marot's sketch shows how the northern, Kingston Avenue, was aligned on the spire of All Saints' church, Kingston. Henry Wise, Queen Anne's gardener, refers to 'a great hill in Kingston avenue which much obstructed the view from the house and gardens and was thought proper to be levelled'. It was intended by William that the southern, Ditton Avenue, would also have an eyecatcher and in about 1699 William Talman designed a Trianon to be built at Long Ditton, but this was never implemented.

8. Johann Zoffany: *A view in Hampton garden with Mr and Mrs Garrick taking tea* (1762). Collection of Lord Lambton

DAVID GARRICK'S VILLA
AT HAMPTON

JOHANN ZOFFANY'S charming paintings of David Garrick's Thames-side villa garden reflect the lifestyle of the man who was perhaps the greatest of England's actors and theatre managers. The pleasures and delights of this riverside Hampton garden were much more relaxed than the more formal would-be Arcadian scenes of Queen Caroline's Richmond gardens or of the Countess of Suffolk's Marble Hill. Zoffany had experienced the Garricks' famous hospitality at first-hand when he stayed with them in 1762; he shows the actor relaxing, rehearsing his lines for the next Drury Lane production, or writing plays and occasional verses, playing with his nieces and dogs, watching his guests fishing from the bank and taking tea with his delightful wife, the dancer Eva Maria, on the lawn by his Shakespeare temple.

The tea urn would have been working overtime when Dr Johnson was a guest. Johnson regarded Garrick's social talents as on a par with his famous natural style acting, but at first barred his election to his literary club on account of the habitual buffoonery and talent for mimicry from which he had himself suffered. The formidable Johnson knew the mercurial 'Davy' as well as anybody; he had been his schoolmaster and together they had left Lichfield to seek their fortunes in London.

The focal point of Garrick's riverside garden was his Shakespeare temple, built in 1755, the year after he had bought the villa. Shakespeare was Garrick's idol and, as a theatre manager, he aimed to restore his plays to favour and to discredit the Restoration playwrights. Inside the temple he placed a life-size statue of the poet by Roubiliac, which is now in the British Museum. Wine flowed freely in the temple where visitors had to pay homage to Shakespeare and were encouraged to write verses in his honour. On May Day Garrick dispensed money and cake to the poor children of Hampton from his special President of the Shakespeare Club chair. According to Horace Walpole, this chair, designed by William Hogarth and seen in his portrait of Mr and Mrs Garrick painted in 1757, had on its back a medal of the poet carved out of a piece of the mulberry tree which Shakespeare had planted at New Place in Stratford. This had been cut down in 1756 and souvenirs sold from it.

Hogarth, who had acquired a villa in Chiswick in 1749, was David Garrick's good friend and kindred spirit. He was the first artist to paint scenes from plays and he painted Garrick in various parts, including his famous Richard III which is in the Walker Art Gallery, Liverpool. Garrick greatly admired Hogarth and his bent for social satire. He owned many of his paintings, including the four election paintings, which hung in the Bow Room of the villa. It was Garrick who wrote the epitaph for Hogarth's tomb at Chiswick on his death in 1764.

Hogarth's book *The Analysis of Beauty*, which was finally published in 1753, had been talked over for some time with his friends, who had been curious to know the reason for the serpentine Line of Beauty which he had painted on his palette in his self-portrait of 1745. Ideas of taste fluctuated, he explained, and his analysis set out to establish what forms and shapes were universally pleasing. Serpentine lines were, he maintained, the most acceptable forms of grace and were the underlying principle of beauty in life and art. The S curve dominated Georgian ideas in furniture and decoration, as shown on the title-page of his book, where also can be seen the curving lines of the petals, stamens and tendrils of Dutch tulips, irises and honeysuckle. Nature's curves soon became the inspiration of mid-century landscape gardening.

Following the turning away from formality earlier in the century, Batty Langley, the Twickenham gardener, had written in his *New Principles of Gardening* in 1728: 'nor is there anything more shocking than a stiff regular Garden', and, in what he called the 'arti-natural' line (which the landscape gardener Stephen Switzer had also promoted as 'natura-linear'), paths began to resemble the fanciful scrollwork of parterres. William Mason in his long poem *The English Garden* (1772-81), records how the early landscapists, in their efforts to abandon straight lines, had fallen into these 'false extremes' until rectified by Hogarth's true line of grace, that 'peculiar curve, alike averse to crooked and to straight'. Mason, friend and gardening ally of Walpole, was one of the first to use 'the general curve of Nature' for perimeter walks, bordered by evergreens and flowering shrubs, ideal for his type of rectory garden:

Smooth, simple path! whose undulating line

With sidelong tufts of flow'ry fragrance crown'd.

'Plain in its neatness', spans my garden ground.

Garrick, Walpole and the writer Richard Owen Cambridge, who were friends and neighbours, were all in the throes of laying out their newly-acquired villa gardens when Hogarth's *Analysis of Beauty* was published, and serpentine walks in the line of beauty began to span the garden ground at Hampton, Strawberry Hill and Twickenham Meadows. Walpole's serpentine walk bordered by flowering shrubs (see *pages 59-64*) was well advanced in the autumn of 1753 and in 1755 he was writing that he 'had contracted a sort of intimacy with Garrick, who is my neighbour. He affects to study my taste'. The following year he was taking cypresses over to adorn the lawn outside Shakespeare's temple and discussing garden improvements with his neighbour, whose wife he found 'all sense and sweetness'. Walpole even extended the rare privilege of publishing Garrick's *To Mr Gray on his Odes* in 1757 on his own new Strawberry Hill Press, the first fruits of which had been Gray's *The Bard and The Progress of Poesy*.

9. *A view of the seat of the late David Garrick, Esq*. Engraving for *The Modern Universal British Traveller* (1779).

Garrick and Walpole watched the progress of Owen Cambridge as he transformed the walled and enclosed gardens of Twickenham Meadows (later known as Cambridge Park), which he had acquired in 1751. Mrs Henrietta Pye, a local resident, admired the way Cambridge's improvements had opened up the river banks as a promenade and picnic ground and she particularly liked the turfed serpentine walk through the grove which ran along the upper part of the Meadows for about three-quarters of a mile, 'winding in and out' and bordered by thick rose bushes, mock orange, lilacs, honeysuckles and sweet williams. A striking adjunct for a landscape park appeared in 1777 when James Paine, who had designed bridges in landscaped gardens, built Richmond bridge, prompting Walpole to call Cambridge 'Mr Foot of the Bridge'.

Neither Walpole nor Garrick had the advantage of Cambridge's direct access to the river. The difficulty with the layout of Garrick's garden, as with several others in the area from Twickenham to Hampton, was that a road separated the garden immediately around the house from the riverside lawn. Garrick had proposed a bridge across, but 'Capability' Brown was called in in about 1756 and advised a grotto-tunnel as Pope had used at Twickenham. On hearing the solution Johnson apparently said approvingly: 'David, David, what can't be over-done, may be under-done'. The tunnel proved a challenge for the playwright John Home who spent a day at Garrick's villa in 1759 with Robert Adam and his brother and a set of golf clubs. Home drove his ball through the tunnel in three strokes, but it had to be retrieved from the river by Garrick who kept it as a memento.

Brown, who had moved to Hammersmith, then a riverside hamlet, in 1751, after leaving Lord Cobham's service at Stowe, was building up his own practice at the time. He remained at Hammersmith until 1764 when he moved to Wilderness House, Hampton Court, the official residence of the royal gardener. It is clear that Brown and Garrick became close friends and on one occasion Garrick wrote to Cambridge that he envied Brown's genius and doted on the man, but how much advice Brown gave Garrick on the laying out of his garden is a matter of speculation. Some of the moulded landform either end of the tunnel could possibly be Brown's work.

There is no doubt, however, that Walpole, Garrick and Cambridge had their own ideas on landscaping, which would have been shared with 'Capability' Brown, who is said to have admired Cambridge's improvements at Twickenham Meadows. But it was Cambridge who is remembered as saying that he hoped he would get to Heaven before Brown had assessed its capabilities for improvement. At the time Brown was working for the Duke of Northumberland at nearby Syon, where by 1754 Hogarth's serpentine line of beauty was much in evidence. Brown was also active at neighbouring Syon Hill for the Earl of Holdernesse working on a winding shrubbery perimeter walk. Holdernesse was William Mason's patron and he was acting as his secretary in 1753 / 4 when Brown was most likely to have been working there. In 1758 both the Duke of Northumberland and the Earl of Holdernesse were signatories to a petition to George II recommending Brown, whose 'Abilities and Merits' they were also fully acquainted with, as a royal gardener (see also *pages 105-6*).

Garrick could not resist making fun of the seriousness of the zeal for landscape gardening at a time when *The World*, a new and influential publication owned by Robert Dodsley which ran from 1753-56, was doing likewise. The chief contributor to these satires of contemporary fashions was Cambridge, with the occasional anonymous essay from Walpole. Essay Number 15, a parody of Squire Mushroom's villa – one of those growing up round London which 'swarm more especially on the banks of the Thames' – reported that 'a great comic painter has proved, I am told, in a piece every day expected, that the line of beauty is an S' and that nothing henceforth would now please the modern gardener that was not serpentine.

In 1757 Garrick introduced into his play *Lethe or Aesop in the Shades*, first produced in 1740, the character of Lord Chalkstone, a gouty peer, who complained as

10. *Mr and Mrs Garrick by the Shakespeare Temple at Hampton* painted in 1762 by Johann Zoffany. Collection of Lord Lambton

he was waiting to cross the Styx into the Elysian Fields that it was laid out without taste and should have a 'serpentine sweep' to improve its 'capabilities'. The part of Chalkstone, played by Garrick himself, was one of his favourites. He never failed to get applause when he advanced to the edge of the stage and peering down into the orchestra, as it were across the ha-ha, called it 'a most curious collection of evergreens and flow'ring shrubs'.

Garrick's most famous words on the serpentine line occur when Mr Sterling's improvements are discussed in *The Clandestine Marriage*, the play which took London by storm in 1766: 'Ay, here's none of your strait lines here – but all taste – zig-zag – crinkum-crankum – in and out – right and left – to and again – twisting and turning like a worm, my Lord'. Zoffany's painting of *The Clandestine Marriage* (now in the Garrick Club) shows Lord Ogleby on a riverside walk with the spire of a parish church in the distance, Mr Sterling having assured him that: 'One must always have a church, or an obelisk, or a something to terminate the prospect, you know. That's a rule of taste, my lord'. In Garrick's case it was the obelisk spire of the parish church across the river at East Molesey that performed this fortunate service.

Garrick's death in 1779, in Johnson's words, 'eclipsed the gaiety of nations', and certainly there were no more scenes at Hampton House such as Zoffany had painted; but his wife lived on until 1822, maintaining the garden as she and her husband had known it and pointing out to visitors the trees they had planted themselves. She would doubtless have often recalled Dr Johnson's own praise of their beloved Thames-side retreat: 'Ah David, it is the leaving of such places that makes a deathbed so terrible'. Garrick's Villa, so-called by his successor and now converted into flats, retains the elegant appearance of Robert Adam's 1775 classical building and the riverside lawn is now a public open space, maintained by Richmond Borough Council. There is a proposal to bring back the layout seen in the 1838 plan, which relates to the engraving of 1779, where Walpole's cypresses have matured and a gravelled serpentine path bordered by shrubberies, which are known to have included 'syringas and lilacs' and 'choice American shrubs', meanders at the back of the lawn. It would be interesting to feature at Garrick's Villa on the banks of the Thames such a clear association with his friend Hogarth's line of beauty and grace.

11. *Map of Garrick's Villa* from a sale catalogue of 1822. London Borough of Richmond upon Thames

A Royal Privy Garden
by the Thames

Close by those meads, for ever crown'd with flowr's,
Where Thames with pride surveys his rising tow'rs,
There stands a structure of majestic frame,
Which from the neighb'ring Hampton takes its name.

HAMPTON COURT relates intimately to the rural Thames, in a way that no other royal palace does, as Alexander Pope well appreciated. Its 'majestic frame' of Tudor and Wren architecture, its Privy Garden, now being restored, Banqueting House and park can all be seen from the towpath or a boat on the Thames. The glories of its buildings and gardens, through the centuries, were entirely dependent on the sovereign's personal regard for Hampton Court, and as far as the Privy Garden was concerned, the amount of royal time spent at the palace.

Henry VIII, who had acquired his palace from Cardinal Wolsey, had a great affection for the place and built a new Great Hall and a Water Gallery by the Thames. Wolsey's knot gardens were transformed into a riverside Privy Garden with scores of royal emblems and a triangular mount garden built with a foundation of a quarter million bricks and surmounted by a three-storeyed Great Round Arbour, to look out over the hunting park and the Thames landscape.

Charles I also delighted in the rural retirement of Hampton Court and planned a grander layout for the park and gardens. Time ran out for him, however, and it was left to Charles II, who had had experience in exile of French gardens with their extended perspectives, to introduce the grand manner to Hampton Court at the Restoration. Before that time Evelyn said the park was 'a flat, naked piece of Ground'. The riverside Privy Garden, with its Tudor mount, did not receive the same grand treatment, however, as the king had little need to use it, preferring to stay at Windsor and merely using Hampton Court for occasional ceremonies. The palace and gardens had unpleasant memories as Oliver Cromwell had spent weekends there and much enjoyed walking in the Privy Garden. The Protector had even had Queen Henrietta Maria's great Arethusa fountain by Le Sueur transferred there from Somerset House.

The heyday of Hampton Court as a royal palace arrived when the Dutch King William and his wife Queen Mary made it their principal residence in 1689 and directed Christopher Wren to modernise the Tudor buildings. To complement his new east front façade Wren retained the main elements of Charles II's scheme, the *patte*

12. *A view of Hampton Court* by Leonard Knyff (*circa* 1702, detail).
The Royal Collection © Her Majesty The Queen

d'oie and the Long Water canal, but the king, not satisfied with grand spatial concepts alone, employed Daniel Marot, whom he brought with him from Holland, to design elaborate parterres to fill in the great semicircle. The motifs of the scrollwork echoed his other decorative designs, particularly those of the king's Delft vases. In the smaller Privy Garden the king demolished the old Tudor mount and used the soil to raise terraces on each side to look down on a new cut-turf parterre.

Daniel Defoe praised William III for having revived 'the love of gardening' in his kingdom. Pepys had noted the Restoration fashion for gardens was 'to make them plain' and in his *Systema Horticulturae* in 1677 John Worlidge lamented the tendency for owners to banish 'out of their gardens Flowers, the Miracles of Nature, the best ornaments that were ever discovered to make a Seat pleasant'. William and Mary, who had been enthusiastic gardeners at their Het Loo palace, gave great encouragement to horticulture and to the nursery trade by their example at Hampton Court and soon, as Defoe pointed out, 'gentlemen followed every where, with such a gust that the alteration is indeed wonderful through the whole kingdom; but nowhere more than in the two counties of Middlesex and Surrey, as they border on the River Thames'.

Although their Majesties were a gardening team and 'both ordered everything that was done', Mary was the botanical gardener and appointed Dr Leonard Plukenet as her personal botanist superintendent. Her passion was for 'curious' or exotic flowers and she encouraged the collecting of rare plants. There were new opportunities for obtaining plants through the Dutch trade with the East Indies, Japan, and the Cape. The *Agapanthus africanus* was seen growing at Hampton Court in 1692.

Queen Mary established herself in the riverside Water Gallery and had the Tudor pond garden area beside the Privy Garden 'laid out into small inclosures, surrounded with Tall hedges to break the Violence of the Winds'. She also had a so-called 'glass-case' garden where she grew her special florists' flowers: auriculas, polyanthuses, finely striped tulips and Marvel of Peru. The queen always had cut flowers in the royal apartments arranged as in Dutch paintings.

King William set the fashion for evergreens, which Defoe said His Majesty thought were 'the greatest addition to the beauty of a garden, preserving the figure of the place, even in the roughest part of an inclement and tempestuous winter'. The lower part of Wren's building leading on to the terrace above the Privy Garden was made into an orangery for wintering the king's tender greens, his Dutch bays, phillyrea, myrtles, oleander, alaternus, and orange and lemon trees.

Queen Mary died in 1694 and William lost interest in the gardens she had so loved, but when Whitehall Palace was virtually burned down in 1698 he made preparation for Hampton Court to become not only his principal residence again but a palace in which to receive the Court. The Broad Walk and the Pavilion Terrace stretching along the Thames to a new bowling green were made for the courtiers to stroll along

13. Jean Tijou's design for wrought-iron
screens at Hampton Court.
Victoria and Albert Museum, London

and were hailed by Stephen Switzer as 'the noblest work of that kind in Europe'. This garden terrace to view the river scenery predated Queen Caroline's famous viewing terrace at Richmond by twenty years.

King William now needed expanded private gardens, not only owing to increased activity at the palace, but because the Treaty of Ryswick in 1697 brought a respite from the European wars he had been engaged in since his accession. Hitherto he had been forced to spend all his summers campaigning and only saw his gardens in the winter, when he consoled himself with his evergreens. The interest in the exotic plant collections died with Queen Mary, but much thought was given to the design of the new Privy Garden.

The Water Gallery was demolished and the Grinling Gibbons carvings set up in a new castellated banqueting house, overlooking the river. The small Privy Garden, now doubled in size, was lowered so that the king could see the barges from the orangery. The Arethusa (or Diana) fountain, which was later set up in Bushy Park, was dismantled and the beautiful wrought iron Tijou screens, originally intended for the Fountain Garden, were erected at the end of the garden. The Privy Garden is now being restored to this 1702 layout and in 1995 visitors will see once again the splendours of the William III garden.

When the overgrown shrubberies were removed the archaeologists found Henry Wise's fleur-de-lys parterre buried underneath and matching perfectly with the Knyff painting of the garden. The precise bedding trenches for the flower borders, the *plates-bandes*, which echo the fleur-de-lys pattern, were revealed. The brick plinths which supported the statues were also found and, along the side terraces, holes spaced sixteen feet apart showed the exact positions of William's clipped evergreens and accorded with a survey now in the Soane Museum.

These topiary works were described by Celia Fiennes in her journal as 'piramids and then round interchangeable'. The alternating dark green obelisk yews contrasting with globes of silver or variegated hollies would have had a striking effect and formed an integral part of the Privy Garden design; a far cry from the Tudor cutwork whimsicalities grown round cane cages described by a sixteenth-century visitor as, 'all manner of shapes, men and women, half men and half horse, sirens, serving maids, with baskets, French lilies and delicate crenellations'.

Fortunately, as these were Royal Works, there is much evidence in the declared accounts of what plants were ordered and what work was paid for in the making of the Privy Garden, which was completed in 1702, the year the king died. We know that 762 yards of box was needed for edging and that over 7,000 bulbs were ordered for the *plates-bandes*. Numbers of standard roses, syringas and honeysuckles were also ordered and these would have been made into the 'round tufts growing upwards' which Celia Fiennes admired so much in William and Mary gardens. Although there is such

14. Hyacinth 'King of Great Britain' named
in honour of King William. This Voorhelm
cultivar had fully double white florets with
red inner petals. The shape is more
graceful than that of modern varieties.
The illustration is by L.M. Seligmann in
Dr Trew's *Hortus nitidissimus* (Vol.1, 1768)

good documentation, there is always difficulty in obtaining the right plants today, but fortunately Het Loo can supply some of the original seventeenth-century bulbs, including Voorhelm's cultivar the fully double *Hyacinthus orientalis*.

For the first time for two centuries it will be possible to see the Wren façade from a distance. The restored Privy Garden will form a self-contained historical ensemble with the royal apartments and orangery and relate to the Tijou screens by the Thames which have hitherto been obscured by shrubberies. The Privy Garden had been simplified by Queen Anne, who had removed all the parterre edgings as she disliked the smell of box, and, in any case, having always detested her brother-in-law, was anxious to change his garden. She only made occasional use of Hampton Court, where, in Pope's famous lines, she would 'sometimes counsel take – and sometimes Tea'.

Bereft of its intricate patterns, the formal shape of the Privy Garden and the clipped evergreens were retained, however, even after Addison and Pope had campaigned against mathematical topiary as 'deviations from Nature'. Many visitors to England in the mid-century were amazed to find that Hampton Court, which had hitherto led the country's gardening fashions, had nothing to show of the much-vaunted English landscape style. 'Capability' Brown, when he became royal gardener and lived at Wilderness House in 1764, was asked by George III to undertake landscape improvements but declined to do so, it is said, 'out of respect to himself and his profession'. His decision was probably influenced by his near neighbour and friend across Bushy Park, Horace Walpole, who, as an antiquarian, in spite of his advocacy of landscape gardening, favoured historic settings and associations.

George III never lived at Hampton Court, preferring Richmond Lodge and Windsor, and Brown continued to maintain the royal garden as he found it. He could not, however, bring himself to clip the yews and hollies formally and Thomas Jefferson noted in his journal that, just after Brown's death, they were running completely wild. It was left to the historian Ernest Law, who lived at the Bowling Green House, to make an appraisal of Hampton Court's garden history in 1890 and to undertake appropriate restoration of the gardens.

Ernest Law was responsible for reviving old names that had gone into disuse – the Pond Garden, the Tiltyard, and the Wilderness – and for the layout of the present Pond Garden and knot garden. His historical revival schemes included clipping the vastly overgrown yews in the Fountain Garden into the giant cones which can be seen today. When Queen Victoria opened the palace to the public in 1838, the Privy Garden was planted with shady flower-bordered walks for 'Grace and Favour' residents, whose children for generations delighted to play peek-a-boo with their nannies in the overgrown shrubberies. Some years ago, when the decision was finally taken to restore the garden, cuttings were taken from the overgrown but original yews and hollies so that they could be renewed as evergreens to 'give figure' to King William's Privy Garden.

KINGSTON

4

N

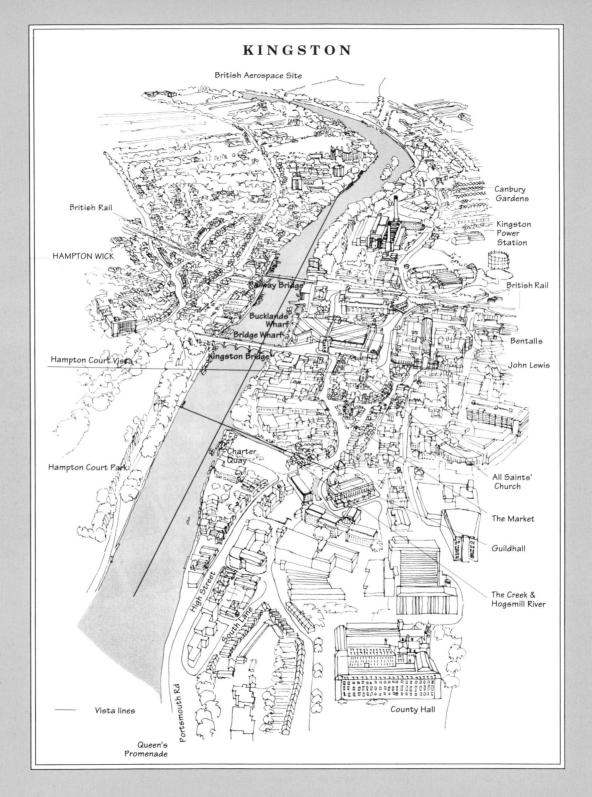

British Aerospace Site

Canbury
Gardens

British Rail

Kingston
Power
Station

HAMPTON WICK

British Rail

Railway Bridge

Bucklands
Wharf

Bentalls

Bridge Wharf

John Lewis

Hampton Court Vista

Kingston Bridge

Charter
Quay

Hampton Court Park

All Saints'
Church

The Market

Guildhall

The Creek &
Hogsmill River

High Street

South Lane

Portsmouth Rd

—— Vista lines

County Hall

Queen's
Promenade

KINGSTON

Landscape and natural history

The Kingston reach covers the historic waterfront of the town, running along the Surrey bank from the end of the Queen's Promenade to the Kingston railway bridge. On the Middlesex bank, there are two distinct landscapes. South of Kingston bridge, mature trees and parkland stretch right to the edge of the Barge Walk. Beyond Kingston bridge, wharves, timber yards, offices and apartment blocks show a complete change of use and character.

At the southern entrance to Kingston, the Portsmouth Road swings right down to the river's edge, terminates the Queen's Promenade and becomes the High Street. Four-storey office buildings and a lone young ash tree mark the entrance to the town, contrasting with the row of two-storey houses along South Lane. The vacant garage site and the mature street plane trees mark the end of the sequence of large Portsmouth Road houses and apartments.

Beyond the Queen's Promenade, the river path narrows down to a paved strip along the water's edge. In some places the path is only two metres wide, while in others, it expands to small raised terraces. Offices, restaurants and boat-clubs front directly on to the path, creating a lively urban edge to the river. The buildings are three storeys or less, leaving the view of All Saints' church unobstructed and creating a comfortable relationship between building height and path width. There are still a number of vacant or derelict sites and temporary car parks along the water at Charter Quay which interrupt access along the river edge. Occasional trees and remnants of old railings help to provide character and coherence, but there is scope for making much more of the waterfront. The scattered conifers, shrub beds and coloured concrete paving do little to complement the historic character of the waterfront. A number of alleys connect back to the bustling market centre of Kingston. Mostly the alleys are dingy and forbidding, but The Griffin shows how the connections can be made more welcoming, opening off the attractive Creek. The Hogsmill river which flows into the Thames here creates opportunities for greening the Thames's edge and the Hogsmill's banks. The National Rivers Authority is undertaking a corridor study of the Hogsmill river.

The stone arches of Kingston bridge provide the entrance to the town from the west and the focal centre of the waterfront from the river. The railway bridge beyond seems less distinguished and might be improved by a fresh coat of paint and a livelier colour scheme.

North of Kingston bridge, the John Lewis development changes the whole scale of the town and river frontage. The quality of the design and the use of materials is exemplary, but the size of the building, in combination with the Bentalls multi-storey car park and the power station beyond, has a major impact on the area. Bridge and Bucklands Wharves have become narrow, though well used, strips and the scale and detail of the remaining boatsheds and the pub along Thames-side have become even more important to the character of the remaining waterfront of landing stages and slipways. The areas of temporary car parking on the water's edge detract from the scene.

Across the river in Hampton Wick, the old timber yards and wharves still determine the character of the bank. A Victorian warehouse has been imaginatively converted into offices and two apartment complexes have been built by the railway bridge, but the semicircular corrugated roofs of the sheds and the stacked timber and activity on the wharves continue to provide the main focus for the area. The boats are now largely pleasure cruisers and tourist launches rather than working barges, but the water is still full of activity.

There is a great contrast between the industrial waterfront on the north of Kingston bridge and the tree'd parkland to the south. The Barge Walk is lined by a row of mature and rounded horse chestnuts and backed by a rank of columnar poplars. The trees and open parkland beyond create a rare London view from the built-up town waterfront on the opposite bank. They provide a good natural green edge to the river bank, contrasting with the urban waterfront on the Kingston side where the solid edge has virtually no vegetation.

Historical background

Kingston, set on rising gravelly ground, defended by the river and surrounding marshes, appears to have been settled along the Hogsmill river as early as the Neolithic era. Kingston is first recorded in an Anglo-Saxon charter in 838 and then in 946, when it had become the venue for a number of councils and coronations, was cited by King Edred as 'the royal town where kings were hallowed'. The Coronation Stone still stands on display outside the present Guildhall.

A bridge has existed at Kingston since at least the twelfth century, and until Putney bridge opened in 1729 only London bridge crossed the Thames below Kingston. The town's strategic importance as a key river-crossing has meant that it featured prominently in military campaigns until after the Civil War.

Although Kingston was never a great ceremonial centre after the Saxon period, it retained considerable status. The bishops of Winchester built a hall here in the early thirteenth century and King John, who granted the town its earliest charter, is also believed to have built a residence at Kingston (the thirteenth-century column outside the library is reputed to come from the building). Merton Priory also had a substantial estate in Kingston, including, by 1450, tofts and a large dovecote.

Despite the John Lewis block which has covered Old Bridge Street, Kingston still retains much of the street pattern of a medieval riverside town, with Church Street, the church, the market place, High Street and Thames Street comprising the best preserved such pattern in Greater London. The Clattern bridge over the Hogsmill river is one of the oldest in Britain. The twelfth-century structure is still intact despite various widenings.

With Henry VIII's arrival at Hampton Court, Kingston became a favoured residence for many of his courtiers and these connections continued under Elizabeth. Wolsey had already linked Kingston to Hampton Court with his elaborate conduit system which brought spring water from Combe Hill to the palace. In 1989 English Heritage restored one of the three surviving conduit houses, now in private grounds.

It was only after the Civil War in which the town suffered for its support for the Royalist cause, that Kingston's royal importance declined. But Kingston had always had a prominent function in the local economy quite apart from its ceremonial and social functions. As well as its market and horse fair serving the surrounding countryside – Celia Fiennes noted in the 1690s that Kingston was a 'great Market for Corne... great quantety's of Corn and Malt sold' – the town had a thriving industrial base. As early as 1264-68 Kingston bailiffs supplied 3,800 pitchers to royal residences from the pottery works here. After the bishops had removed to Esher in the fourteenth century, their residence became Kingston's tannery. It was destroyed by fire in 1963. Bark for tanning was in ready supply given the timber traffic from the wharves; the river made transport of hides a simple matter and by the nineteenth century, a third of the country's leather was processed in Kingston and other Surrey centres.

High Street, formerly known as West-by-Thames was the industrial heart of the town. Behind the crowded street on the river there were malt, corn and coal wharves until the mid nineteenth century, and other industries included distilling, brewing, boat building and iron smelting. Turk's, the most famous of Kingston's boatyards, remains on the site where Richard Turk opened his business in 1740. *Three Men in a Boat* sets out from Turk's. The iron posts on the Middlesex approach to the bridge came from Harris's iron foundry, which operated at 66 High Street and Harris's crest can still be discerned on each post. Building materials for the suburban expansion around Kingston continued to come in via these wharves until well into this century.

At the turn of the century, Kingston was a great centre for pleasure boating. The 'Amateur' regatta, which began in 1829, is one of the oldest in the country. There were fashionable riverside gardens at Nuthall's restaurant and the Sun hotel. The former is now occupied by the Gazebo pub, and the two Victorian gazebos still survive. The grandiose façade of Nuthalls can still be seen above the Millets shopfront.

15. On Queen's Promenade at Kingston. Photograph by Lucilla Phelps

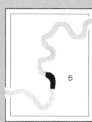

5

HAMPTON WICK

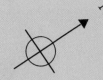

N

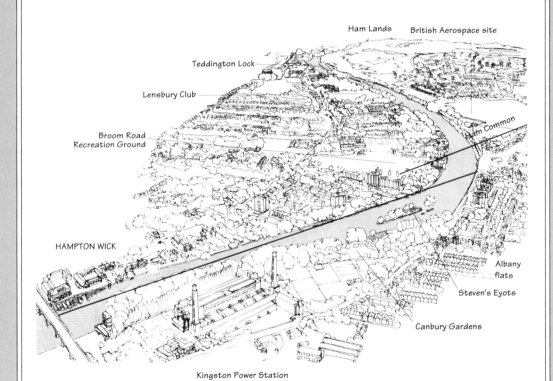

Ham Lands

British Aerospace site

Teddington Lock

Lensbury Club

Broom Road
Recreation Ground

Ham Common

HAMPTON WICK

Albany
flats

Steven's Eyots

Canbury Gardens

Kingston Power Station

——— Vista lines

HAMPTON WICK

Landscape and natural history

The Hampton Wick reach curves from Kingston railway bridge to Teddington lock. The reach is characterised by residential areas interspersed with recreation grounds and dominated by the Kingston power station and British Aerospace site. Yet despite these developments and recent apartment blocks, the reach remains remarkably green and well-tree'd. This leafy character should be enhanced by the recent demolition of the British Aerospace works and the current removal of the redundant power station.

Although the chimneys of the power station can be seen from miles around, huge plane trees and Lombardy poplars reduce some of its impact on the river. Entering the reach from Kingston, the railway bridge and pumping station arches and the lines of trees beyond provide a distinct gateway, leading to the shaded waterside park. The smooth trunks of the plane trees and the high canopy above, create an arcade-like frame to the river. At present, the cracked asphalt, stained concrete street lamps and broken khaki benches leave the place feeling a little uncared for, but the simple space is thronged with walkers and fishermen on the lower path and people just sitting and watching on the upper benches. The river bank at Canbury Gardens, grazed by geese, ducks and other waterfowl, is virtually bare of vegetation. Management could restore the vegetation while still providing a useful area for waterfowl. The bank edges could be stepped to enable birds to move more easily to and from the water. The waterside park leads into the main part of Canbury Gardens, a much-valued and popular park. Though suburban in nature, it has a number of trees providing a sheltered habitat for urban wildlife. A riverside line of trees is backed by strips of shrubberies, a pub and a rowing club. Tennis courts, bowling greens and pavilions occupy the landward edge of the park, creating a dense complex of formal recreation facilities under the shadow of the power station. Some of the tennis courts are covered by inflated white structures in winter. The condition of the chain-link fencing and minimal planting between facilities is deteriorating, though some new planting is underway.

The three other main recreation areas at Broom Road recreation ground, the British Aerospace sports ground and the Lensbury club are largely open areas of gang-mown sports pitches with adjacent pavilions and tennis courts. Broom Road recreation ground presents a hard concrete wall topped by a chain-link fence to the river front. As well as grading and vegetating the river wall, the fence could be set back or indeed removed and the lower part of the recreation land managed as a grassy hay meadow. Particularly on the low Middlesex bank, the glimpses through to open space contrast with the denser tree cover along the rest of the reach. The assortment of exotic trees on the edge of the Lensbury club creates a slightly discordant note in the river landscape of native willow, alder, oak and ash. The area of scrub woodland on the edge of the British Aerospace site blends better with the landscape. However barbed-wire fencing and dumped rubbish on this site detract from its natural character and interrupt the upper river walk to Ham Lands which lie just to the north of the British Aerospace land and are discussed more fully in the Teddington reach (Reach 6). The part of Ham Lands which lies within the Royal Borough of Kingston, comprises riverside grassland with a few bushes and trees. The grassland has been mown regularly in the past and is consequently not as diverse as the grassland cut as a hay crop over the remainder of Ham Lands. There is a range of common grasses, including oat grass on the slope up to Ham Lands, beside the towpath. The remaining grassland is mown regularly. Amongst the grasses can be found wild flowers such as crow garlic, sorrel, yarrow and hardheads. While pathways can be kept closely mown, a late hay cut, with the removal of all the cuttings to avoid fertility build up, would enable more flowers to set seed and thereby ensure their survival and spread.

The residential areas divide into two main types. Downstream of the Albany, Edwardian houses line stretches of the river and its side channels, particularly at Lower Ham Road and Broomwater. The associated domestic boathouses, though often in a state of decay, contribute to the character of the river. The whimsical peaked roofs, barge boards and arched windows of the architecture on the water's edge give the area a special identity. Upstream of the Albany, a number of blocks of flats change the character and scale of the residential areas. The three Albany blocks stand out along the river, built on the site of Point Pleasant with its commanding views to north and south. However the mature cedars, old garden wall and Boston ivy growing on the buildings help to reduce some of the impact. Similarly, riparian trees on the Middlesex bank mask some of the bulk of the modern blocks of flats of up to eight storeys high. From a distance, however, such as the view downstream from the Queen's Promenade, these blocks still stand out harshly in the river scene. Between the flats, opposite Canbury Gardens, a number of older houses with extensive gardens and boathouses offer a softer view across the river.

The trees on the islands also play an important part in the leafy character of the reach. Steven's Eyot is surrounded by houseboats, pilings and a hard concrete edge round its banks, but the pollarded willows help to screen some of the clutter and break the expanse of the reach. There is a tiny island downstream of the Eyot with just a few trees which provide a quiet refuge for birds – cormorants can be seen roosting in the tops of the trees. As with many of the other river islands these two would both benefit from more sympathetic bank treatment and more trees. Though the upper end of Trowlock Island is covered in wooden bungalows, the downstream half is densely wooded with alder, ash and willow, creating a narrow, shaded side-channel where the moored boats all appear

to be painted in a co-ordinated blue and white. Regular mowing has reduced the areas of understorey and the value to wildlife. As the trees start to die and decay they will become more valuable for wood-peckers, but the woodland could be managed to provide a shrub layer, a more natural woodland ground flora, and a more diverse age range of trees.

The islands are dotted with boat clubs. Some of the sheds and club houses are relatively new and brightly painted, others date back at least a century. Some of the finest brick boathouses on Lower Ham Road have been converted into design offices. The ramshackle character of the clubs, surrounded by equipment, masts and hulls, brings the river edge alive with activity.

At the downstream end of the reach, the river is dominated by the tall buildings of the Lensbury club and the television studios, and by the pilings, weirs and rushing water of Teddington lock. At Teddington lock the long narrow island in the centre of the river has a number of trees and demonstrates well how green areas can be built artificially in the river. Although the river is only partly tidal between here and Richmond lock, areas of mud are exposed at low tide and black-headed gulls, mallards, coots and other waterfowl hunt for invertebrate morsels. Sea trout and even salmon swim upstream to breed in the Thames's upper reaches. To assist their migration, Teddington weir has been altered so that they can now gain passage at high tide.

The open expanse of Ham Lands acts as a rough contrast with the manicured Middlesex bank. This southern end of Ham Lands has been narrowed by the residential development which crosses Riverside Drive. However the two-storey houses, 100

metres back from the river, are partly screened by the raised river edge and some thin attempts at tree planting. Where the river bank rises up two short terraces, with parallel paths, there is an opportunity for separating cyclists and pedestrians.

Historical background

The village of Hampton Wick grew up as a hamlet at the point where Kingston bridge crossed over into Middlesex. Its only connection with the village of Hampton, a mile upstream, seems to have been their shared contiguity with Hampton Court and its park. In the Anglo-Saxon period, a single manor of Hampton covered the whole of this peninsula. The lordship was vested by William the Conqueror in Walter de St Valery, who also held Isleworth. The manor remained with the de St Valerys until 1217, shortly afterwards coming to the Knights Hospitallers.

Hampton Wick was one of the many villages and manors amalgamated in the new honour of Hampton Court created in 1539. The honour provided for the making of a new forest or chase for Henry VIII, and was called Hampton Court Chase, 'for the nourishing, generation and feeding of beasts of venery and fowls of warren' and in which the king was to have 'free chase and warren'. The Chase was immensely unpopular as the deer flourished at the expense of crops and other stock and 'the country thereabout in manner made desolate'. After Henry's death, Elizabeth agreed to remove the deer to Windsor Forest.

In three directions Hampton Wick's growth has always been restricted by Bushy Park, Hampton Court Park and the river. Its eighteenth-century seclusion is implicit in the terms of Steele's dedication of the fourth volume of the *Tatler* to the Earl of Halifax from the 'elegant solitude' of his 'little covert' at Hampton Wick. In 1754 Rocque shows only one house, Broom Hall, on the river between Hampton Wick and Teddington. This whole stretch was dominated by the great 260-acre South Field of Teddington. The manor house was owned by the Frederick family between about 1720 and 1820 when the estate was broken up. The house was demolished in the 1930s, but the columns from the doorway were incorporated in the house in Manor Gardens built on its site.

After the South Field was divided up by the Teddington Enclosure Act of 1800, a number of villas were laid out on plots fronting the river, some of them still retaining elegant boathouses. There had also been some development around the Sandy Lane gas works outside Hampton Wick after they were built in 1851, but the land remained predominantly agricultural until the arrival of the railway in 1863. Between 1864 and 1868, development of the old South Field proceeded so quickly that it was known as 'New Found Out'. It later became South Teddington.

On the Surrey side, Canbury Gardens today lie in the shadow of the 1947 power station. In the 1850s, despite the presence of the gas works on the east side of the Lower Ham Road, the area was a tract of marshes and osier beds in which only a solitary cottage stood. Steven's Eyot is named after the boatman who lived there in the late nineteenth century and the site

of the cottage is now a pub. After the arrival of the railway, the land became attractive for industrial use and by 1887 it was an eyesore. The proposal for a public garden was made in terms of a borough motion 'to remove as soon as possible...the tar paving manufactory, the road materials and other miscellaneous and unsavory objects deposited there...that the view from the river shall be a pleasant one and not, as at present, unsightly and obnoxious'. After initial objections on the grounds that a public garden 'would be used by working men', the gardens were laid out to a design by the borough surveyor Henry Macaulay, on topsoil brought in from the nearby reservoir excavations. The park was opened in 1890.

The site of the power station was occupied from about 1877 by the municipally owned Kingston-upon-Thames Fertiliser Department, where raw sewage was toasted in huge ovens to produce a garden fertiliser sold as 'Native Guano'. King's Passage, at the end of Canbury Gardens, was known as 'Perfume Parade' after the filter beds which adjoined the avenue. Despite all this Canbury Gardens were immensely popular, with weekly concerts and beautiful planting. The power station was closed in 1980 and PowerGen began demolition in 1994.

The Bank Farm estate, owned and renamed Point Pleasant by General St John, was the subject in 1796 of a Red Book by Humphry Repton. The proposals included a new house by Nash, the first

completed collaboration by the two men. The scheme's aim was to take advantage of the views both up and down the river, and Repton praised the 'quite new and unexampled' solution which his 'ingenious friend Mr Nash' contrived. This was a house very close to the water's edge, turned at an angle to the river, with the three bows on two fronts. The Repton plan indicates too the undiverted footpath along the river's edge through the estate. By 1899 it was the Albany club, but the house has been demolished and the site is now occupied by three blocks of flats. The raised situation still commands the river bend and the two fine cedars of Lebanon which survive may date back to Repton.

The recently demolished British Aerospace works evolved during the First World War from Sopwith and Hawker's in Kingston. The works were built on part of the Ham Lands, and this southern part of the Lands is now squeezed between the works site to the east and 1960s housing to the north. The housing, Wates's Riverside Estate, swallowed up 60 acres of the Ham Lands in the 1960s, much of it the former Lammas lands whose copyholders forfeited their rights to the Dysart family under the 1902 Act for the Preservation of the View from Richmond Hill. However, the remaining land not already in public ownership was then bought by Richmond Council. After the council had developed five acres in 1983, there was public outcry, leading to the designation of the rest as Metropolitan Open Land.

TEDDINGTON

N

6

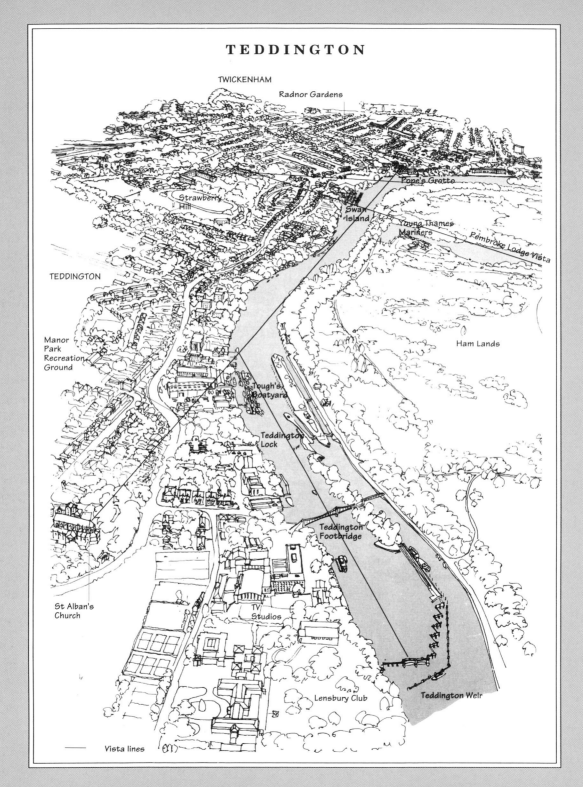

TWICKENHAM

Radnor Gardens

Pope's Grotto

Strawberry Hill

Swan Island

Young Thames Mariners

Pembroke Lodge Vista

TEDDINGTON

Manor Park Recreation Ground

Ham Lands

Tough's Boatyard

Teddington Lock

Teddington Footbridge

St Alban's Church

TV Studios

Lensbury Club

Teddington Weir

—— Vista lines

TEDDINGTON

Landscape and natural history

The Teddington reach is characterised by boatyards and river works interspersed with housing, opposite the wild open space of Ham Lands.

Downstream from Teddington weir the Thames is tidal. Lock works, slipways, docked vessels and boatyards bring the reach alive. The turbulent pool beneath the weirs contrasts with the calmness of the lock where the still water is manipulated from the manicured lawns of the lock-keeper's cottage.

The weir is enclosed by the footbridge and the island and riverbank trees, which help to screen the Thames Television studios and Lensbury club. The brightly painted suspension footbridge is a popular feature with good views of the weir, Tough's boatyard and the fishermen drinking at the end of the Anglers' garden. Just below the lock on the Surrey bank, an obelisk marks the beginning of the Port of London jurisdiction, taking over from the National Rivers Authority which manages the river upstream to the source.

Tough's is the most famous of the boatyards to survive on this stretch, the peeling paint and ramshackle sheds combining with the boats under construction and repair to create a scene of lively river interest and activity. Boat repairs at Ferry Road and Swan Island extend the character throughout the reach.

Between the boatyards, the Middlesex bank has gradually been infilled with private houses and four-storey blocks of flats, sealing Twickenham Road off from the river. Many of the houses are set between 30 and 50 metres back from the water behind mature garden trees. Where the houses are built of brick and tiled, they recede beneath the shade of the trees. White stucco houses with bright orange roofs in treeless gardens are more prominent in the landscape. Garden banks are generally sheet-piled with private cruisers moored at the river's edge.

The only window from the Twickenham Road to the river along this reach is provided by Manor Road recreation ground. The park has some fine mature horse chestnuts, but the close-mown grass and children's dog-free pen do not make the most of the riverside situation.

Strawberry Hill is now cut off from the water by housing developments. A narrow glimpse of the river can still just be seen across Radnor Gardens from Horace Walpole's bedroom. Strawberry Hill now forms part of St Mary's College, but Walpole's original house is currently empty and its future use and public access are being reviewed by the college. Should the funds be raised, there is now a unique opportunity to restore the setting and contents of one of the most significant villas along the Thames, possibly in combination with the neighbouring Radnor Gardens and Pope's Grotto (see Reach 7 and *pages 58-64*). The historic connection between the Waldegraves and the Russells at Pembroke Lodge is retained in the view from Strawberry Hill tower.

Long views from Twickenham and Radnor Gardens look south up the reach to Tough's boatyard and beyond to the roof of St Alban's church. The church has recently been restored and the distinctive green of the copper roof will reappear as the new roof oxidises. Views from Teddington look south-east up the reach, under the footbridge to the weir.

On the Surrey side, Ham Lands provides a complete contrast with the Middlesex bank. The wild open space stretches right round the bend in the river to Ham House and Petersham Meadow, creating one of the most rural parts of the Thames through London. The edges of the area are gradually becoming wooded and managed as coppice with standards and the river banks are gently sloped with gravel beaches or vegetated granite sets. In places the banks have eroded and need repair and scrub has grown up between the towpath and the river and could be cut back, but on the whole the effect is natural and pleasing. The towpath is relatively wooded alongside the southern part of Ham Lands and in managing the trees opportunities could be taken to open up windows to the water. The extra sunlight would benefit the wildlife by promoting new plant growth and small sunny glades. The infilled gravel workings at Ham Lands now support a mosaic of woodland, scrub, grassland and wetland habitats. The site is now a local nature reserve and contains an exceptional diversity of plants and animals, including numerous species which are rare in London.

Ham Lands has been known to local botanists for many years as an important and diverse site. It is particularly famous as one of the only London sites for the nationally scarce Nottingham catchfly, which grew by the towpath until it was overgrown by scrub in the early 1960s. Other plants once found on Ham Lands which are now rare or extinct in London include several species of clover characteristic of dry, sandy soils, common meadow-rue in the flood meadows, autumn squill, and the parasitic great dodder. Although these plants have disappeared, others have colonised the landfill areas, including the rare Deptford pink, which has recently been rediscovered. Over the last ten years over 230 species of plants, including numerous London rarities, have been recorded from Ham Lands, making it one of the richest sites in London.

Hawthorns and willows are scattered throughout the grassland and more extensive areas of scrub and woodland occur, especially to the south near the Thames Young Mariners' base. These areas provide important feeding and nesting cover for birds, including pheasants, stock doves, tawny owls, woodpeckers, spotted flycatchers and six species of warbler, all of which breed on Ham Lands. Foxes, weasels and other mammals also make use of the scrub to hide away during the daytime. However, scrub is spreading into many of the grassland areas and a priority for management would be to check this before the floral diversity of the grassland is lost.

The Young Mariners' base uses an unfilled section of gravel workings within Ham Lands. The still waterbody, gradually becoming surrounded by trees, is well-screened from the river and the lock connection is relatively discreet. The lagoon, connected to the Thames by a sluice, is fringed with willows and provides nesting cover for great crested grebes, mallards, moorhens, coots, swans and reed buntings, all of which breed here despite considerable disturbance from activities such as sailing and angling. Little grebes and kingfishers are both frequent visitors and may breed in some years. The lagoon also contains a good population of fish, together with breeding frogs and toads in spring.

The Young Mariners' building, owned by Surrey County Council, would make an excellent environmental centre combined with its present use. The grassland around the base is kept fairly short and is consequently less diverse, but one area, left unmown until late summer, contains a thriving colony of bee orchids; an indication of the meadow flowers which would grow if the rest of the grassland were to be managed with a late summer hay cut. The sides of the lagoon are steep and there would be great benefit for plants and animals if some areas could be graded to create a wet margin.

Historical background

Teddington's name probably derives from the 'tun' of Tudda's people rather than the more appealing 'tide's end town'. There is no Domesday entry for Teddington and the first direct evidence of the name is in 1100. In the thirteenth century the manor gained independence from the parish of Staines, but it was in the possession of Westminster Abbey when granted to Henry VIII to become part of the honour of Hampton Court. Even after Teddington had been alienated in 1603, the office of bailiff and collector was connected with Hampton Court.

Between the seventeenth and nineteenth centuries Teddington, although never as fashionable as Twickenham, attained a certain popularity with the gentry. Paul Whitehead, poet laureate, the architect Henry Flitcroft and Walpole's friend the artist Richard Bentley are all buried in St Mary's church. Nearly all the houses of the gentry, however, have now been pulled down – Teddington Grove built by William Chambers for Moses Frankes in about 1765, with Chambers's greenhouse and garden temple; Udney House of about 1790, with its Robert Adam picture gallery, demolished as early as 1825; Bushey Villa, possibly by Stephen Wright. By the eighteenth century the High Street was lined with houses, communications having been improved by the turnpiking of the Twickenham road in 1767. However, until the nineteenth century, Teddington remained an isolated agricultural community, with Hounslow Heath to the east, the river to the west and its great open fields to the north and south.

There has been a weir at Teddington since at least 1345, but the present lock was built in 1812. The weir marks the end of the tidal reach of the river. The 1812 structure was one of several built on Rennie's recommendation to improve the notoriously bad navigation. The present enormous barge lock and tiny skiff lock were built in 1950.

Suburban development followed the arrival of the London and Southwestern and the Thames Valley Railways in 1863 - 64. After that, Teddington's population grew enormously, from 1,183 in 1861 to 14,037 by 1901. Development spread rapidly with Upper Teddington west of the station, and southwards from Fulwell station to join up

16. Swan and brood.
Photograph by Lucilla Phelps

with the slightly earlier New Hampton. Along with New Found Out in the south, the new settlements built a church, a cottage hospital, a hotel, shops and a town hall with ballroom and theatre.

Although it brought these amenities the suburban expansion did not include any new industries. As early as 1746 there seems to have been a linen-bleaching works between the north of Broom Road and the river. By 1831 the parish contained 'the largest and most complete establishment... in the kingdom' for wax-bleaching and candle-making. This later became the Paint Research Station. Boat-building had been an important local industry since at least 1855. R.A.Tough opened his famous yard in 1895, and many small boats left from here for Dunkirk in 1940. In the second half of the nineteenth century, market gardening was a major employer and was continuing to employ 200 people as late as 1921.

To the north, Horace Walpole bought the lease on a small house in 1747 on land known as Strawberry Hill Shot. The Gothick confection he built there remains one of the great monuments of the eighteenth century. (For a full account of Walpole's activities as a gardener see *pages 58-64*).

Although some way from the Thames, one of England's most important industries in the eighteenth century, the manufacture of gunpowder, had an impact on the riverside. The industry had a centre on Hounslow Heath, using the river Crane to drive the mills and the willows to supply high quality charcoal in an area that was reasonably remote but convenient for

17. Teddington Lock. Photograph taken in about 1910. London Borough of Richmond

London. Unfortunately the charcoal burning was often in close proximity to the finished product and explosions were common. In 1772 Walpole wrote to his cousin the Hon. Henry Seymour Conway, a lieutenant-general in the Royal Ordnance:

I have been blown up; my castle is blown up; Guy Fawkes has been about my house; and the 5th of November has fallen on the 6th of January! In short, nine thousand powder-mills broke loose yesterday morning on Hounslow Heath; a whole squadron of them came hither, and have broken eight of my painted-glass windows; and the north side of the castle looks as if it had stood a siege. The two saints in the hall have suffered martyrdoms! they have had their bodies cut off, and nothing remains but their heads.

Walpole suggested the powder be kept safely under water until required.

Ham Lands or Ham Fields were settled as early as the Stone Age, and there are remains of an Anglo-Saxon village here, but in medieval times they were a tract of water meadows near the river and open grazing on the poor soils of the flood plain. In 1670 the Duke of Lauderdale made use of them by extending his great east-west avenue across their northern part almost to the river bank. The Rocque maps show the way it was laid out across the old meadows.

18. Part of John Rocque's
survey of London (1744-46)

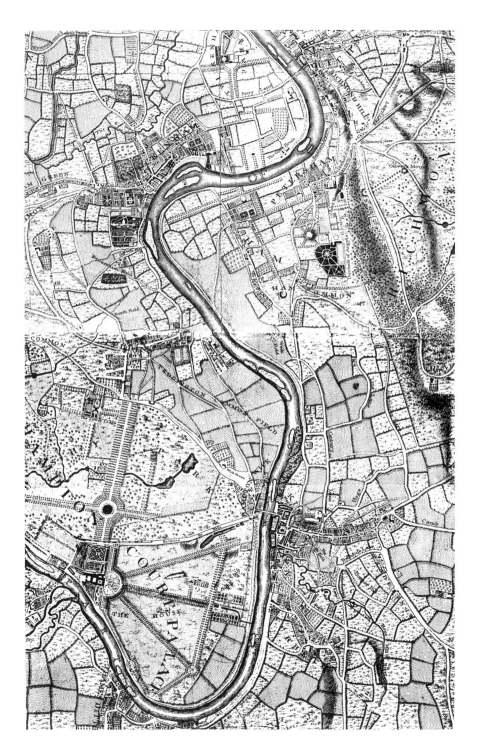

The 1902 Act for the preservation of the view from Richmond Hill involved the extinction of the Lammas rights of many copyholders, although the 1901 plan shows that many copyholders resisted this loss of their ancient rights. Odd narrow strips like Greenwood's aster fields continued to hold out until the 1950s. The Act in fact only preserved a narrow band of the river bank on the northern edge of Ham Lands, and with the Lammas rights extinguished, the land was freed for a massive programe of gravel extraction.

After the construction of the improved Teddington lock in 1904, the frequency of flooding on the Ham Lands declined. In that year, the Ham River Grit company was granted a lease on the Lands, and began extracting gravel which was shipped from a newly constructed works and wharf on the Thames. Gravel had always been extracted in small quantities for local building from the river bank, but the industrial scale of this operation prompted effective protests about the impact on the view from Twickenham and in the 1920s a canal was cut across the towpath to a lagoon where processing and loading could carry on out of sight. At their greatest extent in the 1930s the workings even encroached as far north as the line of the Ham Avenue. After the Second World War, once the entire area had been worked, it was backfilled with enormous amounts of spoil and rubble from bomb-damage and the whole area is now considerably higher than it was at the beginning of the century.

19. *Horace Walpole in his library at Stawberry Hill.* Engraving from a watercolour by J. Muntz (1756)

HORACE WALPOLE
AND THE LANDSCAPING OF
STRAWBERRY HILL

Horace Walpole famous all over Europe for his Strawberry Hill gothic an antiquarian, collector, romance writer, patron of poets and of the Picturesque, was also a 'gardenist' as he termed it. He visited landscape gardens in the making and studied the work of their designers. He had no wish for a grand house set in acres of uninhabited parkland, like his father's at Houghton in Norfolk, but relished the 'animated prospect' of friends' houses at Mount Edgcumbe, overlooking the Tamar, and Mistley with its busy view of the Stour estuary.

He decided in the mid 1740s, after his father's death, that 'Twickenhamshire' was ideal for his requirements but had difficulty in finding a suitable riverside property. A map by John Rocque of 1745 shows the area as he found it. There were the two large estates of Twickenham Park and Twickenham Meadows (later Cambridge Park) and numerous villas in the village of Twickenham with only small grounds, such as that acquired by Pope in 1719. Towards Teddington the Cross Deep area is seen on Rocque still in commonfields (see *plate 18*), presenting Walpole with 'a situation where land is so scarce and villas as abundant as formerly at Tivoli and Baiae'.

However, in 1747 he was able to buy the lease of a small house, known as Chopp'd Straw Hall with a piece of land which was called Strawberry Hill Shot looking out over Twickenham, a 'seaport in miniature', which 'in the setting sun and the long autumnal shades enriched the landscape to a Claude Lorraine'. Having set his heart on a landscaped garden, Walpole immediately began to plant up the five acres of land on which it stood until it 'sprouted away like any chaste nymph in the Metamorphoses'. Permission was obtained to graze in the meadows 'some Turkish sheep and two cows, all studied for their colours for becoming the view'. Fortunately in 1748 Walpole was able to purchase the freehold and four more acres, making his 'territory prodigious' for Twickenham.

In 1750, even before Walpole began to convert the house into his famous 'gothic castle', he turned his attention to creating a terrace the whole breadth of his land 'on the brow of a natural hill' to command the river view. Although he acquired the coveted meadows, where his picturesque animals already grazed, in 1754 and installed a gothic bridge across the ha-ha, it was still some time before he secured the rest of the land down to the Thames. Walpole had to acquire most of his landscape piecemeal and ended up with 46 acres, having negotiated possession of the strip fields, sometimes a rood at a time. On one part there remained right of commonage after the grass was mown, and there is still a narrow right of way under Walpole's former terrace incongruously wending its way with modern lights behind the new houses.

Walpole describes his own 'animated view of the country' and the 'moving pictures' from the windows of Strawberry Hill as:

a gay variety of the scene without, which is very different from every side, and almost from every chamber and makes a most agreeable contrast; the house being placed almost in an elbow of the Thames, which surrounds half, and consequently beautifies three of the aspects. Then my little hill, and diminutive enough it is, gazes up to royal Richmond; and Twickenham on the left and Kingston Wick in the right, are seen across bends of the river, which on each hand appears like a Lilliputian seaport. Swans, cows, sheep, coaches, post-chaises, carts, horsemen and foot passengers are continually in view. The fourth scene is a large common field, a constant prospect of harvest and its stages traversed under my windows by the great road to Hampton Court.

Walpole believed that 'the possessor, if he has any taste, must be the best designer of his own improvements'. When a friend asked him if his garden was going to be gothic like his little castle, the author-to-be of the spine-chilling *Castle of Otranto* made it clear that he had no intention of emulating a gothic novel hero who sought out the 'gloomiest shades as best suited to the pleasing melancholy that reigned in his mind', but, on the contrary, he wanted a garden for Strawberry Hill, which would be 'nothing but riant and the gaiety of nature'.

Walpole's whole attitude to life was influenced by his poet friends, particularly Thomas Gray, who first aroused in him a passion for picturesque scenery, and William Mason, the poet-gardener, who took over as his 'confessor in literature' after Gray's death. William Mason, author of *The English Garden*, transformed the 'gaiety of Nature' of the paradisal gardens of romance into practical gardening ideas. Walpole in his *Essay on Modern Gardening*, a prose counterpart of Mason's long garden poem written at the time of his landscaping of Strawberry Hill and later published by his own printing press in 1771, emphasised the contribution made by poets to the inspiration of the English garden. He saw Milton's description of the Garden of Eden as the prototype of all that was desirable in gardening.

Although Walpole approved of 'modern gardening' and enjoyed his open landscape views, his 'romantic inclinations' craved secluded spots where he could enjoy Milton's blossoming 'wilderness of sweets' and the fragrance of 'flowers worthy of paradise'. For a bower Walpole felt he could do no better than consult Spenser's *Faerie Queene*. One of the romance features which most delighted Walpole and Mason was the tree drapery of trailing garlands of clematis, wild fruits and honeysuckles against a dark canopy of woodland evergreens, where Nature and art went hand in hand and, as the romance writers suggested, Nature might even imitate her own

20. *The Chapel in the Wood.*
Engraving from Walpole's
Description of Strawberry Hill (1798)

21. *South view of Strawberry Hill* (*circa* 1775). Watercolour by Paul Sandby. Ashmolean Museum, Oxford

artful imitations as, in Tasso's words, 'nature played a sportive part / and strove to mock the mimic works of art'. For Mason it was this 'lovely carelessness' of Nature that must be copied, where roses and garden flowers mingled naturally with her wild shrubberies.

In 1753, the year that Hogarth published his ideas on the serpentine line of beauty, Walpole began to plant his enchanted woodland: 'a serpentine wood of all kinds of trees and flowering shrubs and flowers'; and in 1765 he could boast that 'the honeysuckles dangle from every tree in festoons; the syringas are thickets of sweets'. His neighbour Mr Ashe, a nurseryman who supplied him with some of his plants, knew that anything for Strawberry Hill was required to 'hang down somewhat poetical'. It was Mr Ashe's boundary hedgerow, which Walpole bought in 1752, that formed the base of the serpentine wood, where in 1761 he sat up far into the night to listen to the nightingales with Mason and Gray.

Stephen Switzer in his *Ichnographia Rustica* (1718) had pointed out that at a time of enclosure many landowners might inherit hedgerows through which a gravel walk could easily be made, and Walpole knew the Thames-side Wooburn ferme ornée, near Chertsey, called 'Southcote's paradise' by Gray, which had, according to Thomas Whately, a perimeter 'thick and lofty hedgerow, which is enriched with woodbine, jessamine, and every odiferous plant whose tendrils will entwine with the thicket'. Walpole would also have seen this kind of floriferous hedgerow planting at Rousham in Oxfordshire, one of his favourite gardens, where William Kent, who was also greatly affected by Spenser's garden descriptions in *The Faerie Queene*, had instructed the gardener how to plant a romantic 'serpentine walk':

there you see deferant sorts of Flowers, peeping through the deferant sorts of Evergreens, here you think the Laurel produces a Rose, the Holly a Syringa, the Yew a Lilac, and the sweet Honeysuckle is peeping out from under every Leafe, in short they are so mixt together, that youd think every leafe of the Evergreens, produced one flower or a nother.

The effect of the romantic shrubbery walk, with peephole scenes of the gothic castle, must have been that shown on Walpole's bookplate fleuron, which headed his *Essay on Modern Gardening*. Some of these 'hide and discover' views, so beloved of Mason and their mutual friend, William Gilpin, might be recaptured today. This would bring back the spirit of Strawberry Hill even though the open views of Walpole's beloved 'animated scenery' of the Thames have disappeared. It might also be possible to screen the modern buildings by a new serpentine shrubbery, with a solid base of thorn, laurel, ilex, holly, box and privet and a riot of 'every odiferous plant whose tendrils will entwine the thicket'. Then the real Strawberry Hill could feature as a picturesque unit.

Walpole's letters refer to much of the planting, as he even propagated plants himself to distribute to his friends; these included acacias, hypericum, stone pine, almonds, Carolina cherries, Spanish brooms, Chinese arbor-vitae and, with special reference to Strawberry Hill, the arbutus or strawberry tree. We know that he loved his garden best at 'lilac-tide'. Orange trees in pots were arranged around Strawberry Hill and gates and hurdles were painted olive green according to Mason's instructions.

Most of the features that were to be found along the serpentine walk, the shell bench, gothic gate and altar tomb have disappeared, but the chief feature, the Chapel in the Wood, built in 1772, still remains in the north-east corner, but now embedded in college buildings. In the south-east corner of the shrubbery the Waldegrave pavilion makes a new contribution to the scenery. Walpole's smaller gardens, at his cottage across the road and the round flower garden have been developed and there is only a small part of his Prior's garden under the great bedchamber left. However, there is no doubt that it is the restoration of the 'serpentine walk' that would bring back the spirit of the Strawberry Hill of world renown.

Walpole, like Lord Burlington, was a great arbiter of taste. He was one of the first to see the building and the landscape in a picturesque relationship, twenty years before Richard Payne Knight at Downton. He was the first garden historian and his work is of paramount importance. He knew the owners of the gardens he described personally, their fortunes and idiosyncrasies. He was familiar with the work of Bridgeman, Kent and Brown and able to assess their special contributions to the development of landscape gardening; he also appreciated how much amateurs had contributed to the art of 'modern gardening', Southcote at Wooburn Farm, Charles Hamilton at Painshill and particularly his neighbour Pope, who had given poetic inspiration, and the Duke of Argyll at Whitton, who had greatly enriched the landscape by his introduction of foreign trees and plants.

Walpole's own contribution to landscaping anticipated Humphry Repton and Regency ornamental gardening. While admiring naturalised gardens he paused to wonder, at the height of 'Capability' Brown's career, if 'in some lights the reformation seems to have been pushed too far'. Instead of leaving a house 'gazing by itself in the middle of a park', he called for sheltered walks and specialised gardens for the owner's comfort. At Little Strawberry Hill, which he let to Kitty Clive and later to the Berry sisters, treillage features in a sheltered garden were introduced into the communal Strawberry landscape. This approach to landscape gardening would not have escaped Repton's notice when he was personally taken round Strawberry Hill by Walpole.

Walpole's great range of interests and expertise makes him a most perceptive eyewitness of the eighteenth-century landscape movement. Although in his book on *Modern Gardening* Walpole claimed only to be writing a history, Repton acknowledged that 'in his lively and ingenious manner' Walpole had given 'both the history and the rules of art better than any other theorists'.

ALEXANDER POPE
AND THE THAMES LANDSCAPE

ALEXANDER POPE (1688-1744) created a life of classical retirement for himself at Twickenham, much as Horace Walpole was later to induce a medieval habit of mind into his reclusive life at neighbouring Strawberry Hill. But Pope, having suffered a bone disease as a boy which contracted his growth and left him with a humpback, was a permanent invalid; his preoccupation with classical ideas was a way of coping with the many restrictions his deformity and frailty imposed on his activities. His life was necessarily fulfilled by his reading, translations of the classics, writing, friendships, gardening and grotto-making, and everything he did was polished and refined to perfection. Pope was first and foremost a poet, inspired by a lifetime's study of classical writers. The poets Horace and Virgil had celebrated the first Augustan age of peace after a period of civil war; Pope was the epitome of England's own Augustan age of literary eminence.

Pope's 'imitations' of Horace were not antiquarian pieces but attempts at re-creating classical ideas in the contemporary scene to which was added a new topographical note. The traditional scenery of classical pastoral poetry, with its green retreats, lawns and opening glades, sequestered bowers, fauns, birdsong and flowery meadows, was a mixture of the idealised Arcadia of Virgil's *Eclogues* and the Sicilian landscapes of the Greek poet Theocritus which previous imitators had not sought to localise. Pope, however, transferred the classical *'locus amoenus'*, where shepherds and shepherdesses enjoyed their simple idyllic lives, to his native Thames valley.

Throughout his life Pope lived near the Thames: first on the outskirts of Windsor Forest, then briefly at Chiswick as Lord Burlington's neighbour, and from 1718 until his death in 1744 at Twickenham. His only break was the occasional visit to friends' country houses, but for him there were 'no scenes of paradise, no happy bowers, equal to those on the banks of the Thames'. In his first pastoral, composed at the age of sixteen and headed by an appropriate quotation from Virgil on the delights of a sylvan river valley, he wrote:

> First in these fields I try the sylvan strains,
> Nor blush to sport on Windsor's blissful plains:
> Fair Thames, flow gently from this sacred spring.
> While on thy banks Sicilian Muses sing. . . .

22. *An exact Draught and View of Mr. Pope's House at Twickenham*. Engraving by Nathaniel
Parr after Rysbrack (*circa* 1735). London Borough of Richmond upon Thames

> Blest Thames's shores the brightest beauties yield
> Feed here my lambs, I'll seek no distant field.

Twickenham soon became known as the classic village once Pope had settled there. 'The Gods and fate have fix'd me on the borders of the Thames, in the Districts of Richmond and Twickenham', he wrote with satisfaction. He felt at one with Horace and Cicero, who associated their country retreats with contemplative study and poetic composition, and he frequently called his Twickenham retreat 'my Tusculum' after Cicero's villa outside Rome.

All in all, the life and landscape of 'Twickenhamshire', as Walpole called it, was pure Arcadia for Pope. The nymphs and shepherds were no imaginary swains of a golden age but recognizably of Queen Caroline's court at Richmond. At Marble Hill, Henrietta Howard, whom Pope called a 'pastoral lady', the Chloe of his eclogues, entertained literati, including Jonathan Swift and John Gay, at one of Pope's most 'happy bowers' along the Thames. Across the river, the Duchess of Queensberry, who had her portrait painted as a milkmaid and boasted that she could personally milk a cow, gave Gay a summerhouse by the Thames in which to write his poems. Gay, Swift and Pope were a powerful trio, 'the three Yahoos of Twickenham', as Bolingbroke called them, and Pope relished Swift's satire worlds of Lilliput and Brobdingnag.

Pope's eulogy of pastoral simplicity and felicity was reinforced by the architectural cult of the Palladian villa for the man of taste. Lord Burlington, the acknowledged leader of the movement, whom Pope called 'the Apollo of the Arts', was a close friend and neighbour at Chiswick, and when Pope moved to Twickenham the earl was on hand to advise on alterations. Pope, with 'a River at my Garden's end', adapted his house by raising a portico on the floor above his grotto entrance to take advantage of the moving river scenery as enjoyed by the Palladian villas on the Brenta.

Condemning the 'capricious ornaments' of baroque architecture, Colen Campbell, who was later to design Marble Hill, had promoted the 'simplicity of antiquity' as the right model in his *Vitruvius Britannicus* (1715-25) and Pope followed by calling for this 'amiable simplicity' of the 'taste of the ancients' to be copied in gardens as well. Horace's frequently quoted classical theme of *simplex munditiis* was the aim, the right balance between nature and art, when the designer shunned artificial ornaments in favour of Nature's own materials. The phrase, translated by Milton as 'plain in its neatness', was taken from the imagery of the modest fair Roman youth who neither wore false ornaments nor left his hair unkempt, but simply braided his tresses elegantly. Pope had already dwelt on this interpretation of simplicity in the preface to the *Iliad* when he had defined it as 'the mean between Ostentation and Rusticity' and returned to the *simplex munditiis* theme in 1731, when, in his *Epistle to Lord Burlington*, he advised with reference to gardening:

In all, let Nature never be forgot.
But treat the Goddess like a modest fair
Nor over-dress, nor leave her wholly bare.

Pope's plea for the 'simplicity of unadorned nature' came to be interpreted in different ways, but for him it was not an anticipation of the naturalised mid-century landscaped gardens. Nature was to be dressed, but not overdressed, with green amphitheatres, wilderness groves, quincunxes, colonnades, terraces, mounts and subterranean grottoes. 'Beauties not forced into it but resulting from it'. He, like Addison, particularly condemned the artificiality of topiary as 'deviations from Nature'.

Pope was said to be 'the contriver' of Henrietta Howard's garden at Marble Hill, although the royal gardener Bridgeman was professionally involved. A drawing by Augustin Heckel of 1748 shows the neat stepped down effect as seen from a boat on the river, but a recently discovered survey shows a detailed garden plan which can be compared with the conjectural classical garden, Pliny's Tuscan Villa, from Robert Castell's *The Villas of the Ancients Illustrated* (1728), with its hippodrome-shaped green space and semicircular arcade of trees, quincunxes and to the side an irregular wilderness. The latter was 'the imitation of the natural face of the country', Pliny's *imitatio ruris*, which Castell claimed to be the classical authority for irregularity in gardens. *The Villas of the Ancients Illustrated* had been influenced by the ideas of Castell's patron Burlington and by Pope's classical scholarship.

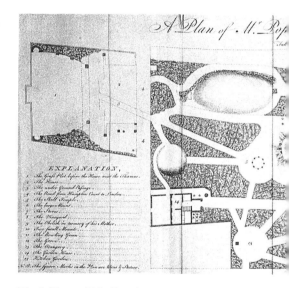

23. *A Plan of Mr. Pope's garden as it was left at his Death* by John Serle (1745)

Pope's own garden was extremely influential on landscape gardening, although still adhering to the 'neatness' of Horace's 'modest fair' tradition. The larger part of Pope's garden, as shown in John Serle the gardener's plan of 1745 prepared for visitors, was across the public highway with a tunnel connecting it with the riverside lawn; the entrance under the portico can be seen in a picture of the villa. The shell temple at the garden side of the grotto tunnel entrance was built by William Kent, who had illustrated Calypso's grotto in Pope's *Odyssey*.

Pope contrived a number of 'pleasing intricacies' in a small space: an arcade, a bowling green, a mount, a vineyard, quincunxes measured out by Lord Peterborough, and a theatre made by Bridgeman's labourers spared from Richmond by the Princess of Wales. He used the rules of painting he had learnt from the artist Charles Jervas and gave greater distance to his short alleys by darkening and narrowing the planting. He also worked out the psychology of literary and emotional associations in relation to visual effects, inducing melancholy or cheerful moods by various planting. After his mother's death in 1733, he erected an obelisk in her memory at the end of a solemn cypress walk. It much impressed Walpole.

Walpole said of Pope that 'of all his works he was most proud of his garden', and that 'it was a singular effort of art and taste to impress so much variety and scenery on a spot of five acres'. The layout, although ordered in its variety, was a far cry from the axial squared gardens of the Kneller estate at Whitton or the gardens of New Park, Petersham as seen on the engravings by Kip. Pope's garden was entered obliquely from the tunnel and the various irregular-shaped components opened up as surprises rather than being seen at a glance on a rectangular plan. Lord Burlington's garden at Chiswick, which, unlike Pope's, can still be seen today, is a grander version of the poet's classical garden at Twickenham.

The principles that governed both gardens are revealed in Pope's *Epistle to Lord Burlington* of 1731:

> Let not each beauty ev'ry where be spy'd,
> Where half the skill is decently to hide.
> He gains all points, who pleasingly confounds
> Surprizes, varies and conceals the Bounds.

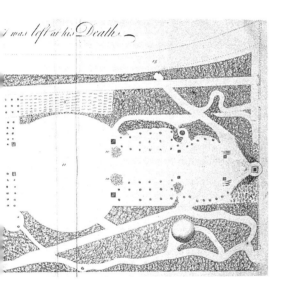

24. *A view in Pope's garden at Twickenham* sketched by William Kent (*circa* 1725-30). British Museum, London

Pope's neat, polished remarks have the force of proverbs: 'Fools rush in where angels fear to tread'; 'A little learning is a dangerous thing'; 'Hope springs eternal in the human breast', to recall a few. His landscape pronouncements, in the same way, became rallying cries for those laying out great country estates. 'Consult the Genius of the Place in all'; 'Let Nature never be forgot'. What Pope had shown 'in miniature', in his friend the poet James Thomson's words, had given the landscape movement its first green shoots. Walpole, who maintained that landscape gardening was chiefly influenced by poetic sensibility, felt that Pope had been a direct influence on William Kent, whom he saw as the 'father of modern gardening'.

Walpole, who arrived in Twickenham three years after Pope's death, deplored the treatment of Pope's garden by his successor Sir William Stanhope. He lamented that he had 'hacked and hewed' the 'sacred groves' and 'wriggled a winding gravel walk through them with an edging of shrubs, in what they call the modern taste'. Interestingly enough, the serpentine flowery shrub walk was the modern taste that Walpole particularly approved of elsewhere in the gardens of Thames villas, including his own Strawberry Hill. Walpole's strong sense of history, however, dictated that 'some monuments of our predecessors ought to be sacred', and he could only regret that the little compartments the poet had 'twisted and twirled and rhymed and harmonized' as intricately and painstakingly as his verses, should now be opened up and exposed so that 'if the Muses wanted to tie up their garters, there is not a nook to do it in without being seen'.

Although Pope's villa itself was destroyed in 1807 and part of his famous garden has now been developed, the underground grotto has miraculously survived. Pope, who had studied perspective with the painter Jervas, spent hours in his grotto, which was lined with shells, sparry marble from Mount Edgcumbe, amethysts, lava from Vesuvius, and pieces of glass in angular forms which reflected sails on the river and trees in a camera obscura effect. At its entrance he placed an inscription from Horace, who also had a grotto at his Sabine Farm: '*Secretum iter, et fallentis semita vitae*'. One visitor's translation seems to reflect the pleasure and inspiration Pope's grotto gave him:

> A hid Recess, where Life's revolving Day
> In sweet Delusion gently steals away.

It is to be hoped that this important piece of literary and garden heritage will one day be restored.

25. *View of Pope's Villa at Twickenham during its Dilapidation* painted by Turner in 1808. Reproduced by kind permission of Sudeley Castle, Winchcombe, Cheltenham, Gloucestershire

7

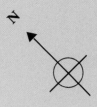

N

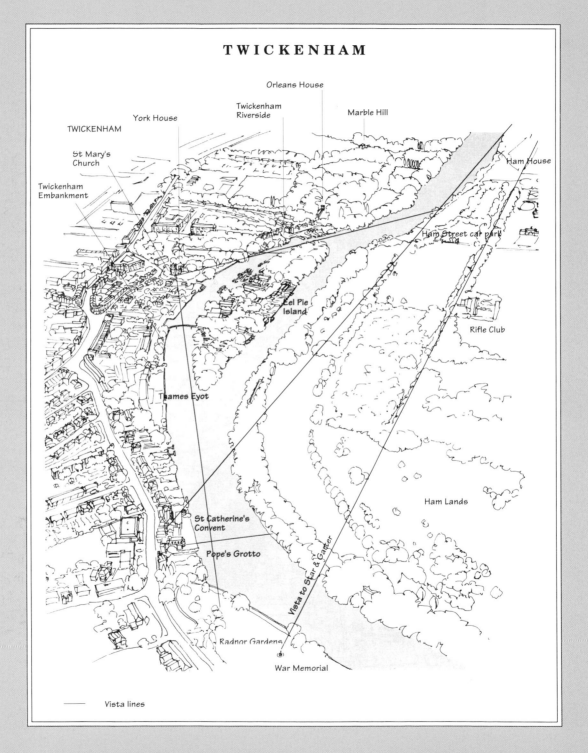

TWICKENHAM

Orleans House

Twickenham
Riverside

Marble Hill

York House

TWICKENHAM

St Mary's
Church

Ham House

Twickenham
Embankment

Ham Street car park

Eel Pie
Island

Rifle Club

Thames Eyot

Ham Lands

St Catherine's
Convent

Pope's Grotto

Vista to Star & Garter

Radnor Gardens

War Memorial

—— Vista lines

TWICKENHAM

Landscape and natural history

Twickenham is one of the classic Thames waterfronts, with church and historic buildings clustered around wharves and boatyards. The Twickenham reach runs along the Middlesex bank from Radnor Gardens through the Embankment to the Riverside. Eel Pie Island encloses the historic waterfront, separating Twickenham from the wild expanse of Ham Lands on the Surrey banks.

Radnor Gardens has become a popular local park, with an active residents' support group. Though Radnor House was hit by a bomb in 1940 and demolished, part of the foundations and one of the garden pavilions remain. Part of the garden originally lay on an island, but the river channel gradually became clogged with rubbish and was filled and grassed over in the 1970s. A well used bowling green and a new pavilion have been added to the park and the Friends of Radnor Gardens are currently looking at ways of improving the park's layout, seating, safety, performance spaces, screening from the road and views to the river.

Radnor Gardens are set on a particularly significant spot. Not only does the park provide one of the only windows from the built-up Middlesex banks on to the river, it also acts as the focal point for the Ham House Avenue, visually linking Richmond Hill with Twickenham. The park's war memorial was originally placed there to be seen at the end of the avenue by the disabled soldiers and sailors in the Star

and Garter Home on the hill. Further significance comes from the park's location between Pope's Grotto and Strawberry Hill. The redesign of the park, coinciding with the possible reinstatement of the main Ham avenue and the settings of Strawberry Hill and Pope's Grotto, would have a dramatic impact on this part of the river, restoring connections across one of the most influential landscapes in the history of the English Landscape Movement.

In the seventeenth century the Dysarts planted a bold grid of lime avenues across Ham Lands. Most of these avenues have survived through three centuries to the present day. The main east-west avenue even largely weathered the period of twentieth-century gravel extraction and it has only been in the last twenty years that the western end has disappeared under sycamore and elm scrub growth. A firing range intrudes into a short section of the avenue line. Scrub is gradually obscuring views and access across the public open space and invading the floristically rich grassland. A Countryside Commission stewardship agreement with the London Borough of Richmond is tackling the control of scrub growth and the management of the grasslands. Glimpses from the towpath back into Ham Lands are being reopened by a programme of coppicing. The management of this scrub growth by coppicing lengths will keep the elm healthy (by keeping elm under 20 cm in diameter at breast height it is less vulnerable to Dutch elm disease),

will link the habitat of the meadow with the river habitat, and will create sunny glades to add habitat diversity and encourage plants and invertebrates. This reach includes an important section of Ham Lands, the nature conservation interest of which is described on *pages 53-54*.

One of the glimpses to be reopened would be the vista from Pope's Grotto across the river into the landscape which inspired his writings. The Grotto is the only part of Pope's Villa to survive, but its connection to the river has been blocked by a science laboratory built in 1934. The grotto and neighbouring tea merchant's house are now owned by St Catherine's Convent and the school which shared the buildings has recently moved across the road into new premises in Pope's old garden. The laboratory is vacant and, depending on the nuns' plans, it may eventually be possible to remove the 1934 structure and restore the connection with the river. Should the convent buildings come up for sale in the future and adequate funding be secured, it may even be possible to convert the site into a study centre, at what was the heart of the eighteenth-century English Landscape Movement (for more on Pope see *pages 65-71*)

The tower of St Catherine's Convent, said to be designed in the shape of a caddy by the tea merchant builder, stands out as a landmark on the river from as far as Petersham Meadow. The surrounding area has been intensively developed as private housing, but the buildings are generally less than three storeys and the tower stands out above the trees of Ham Lands.

Downstream from the convent, private houses line the Middlesex bank as far as the Twickenham Embankment. The gardens are between twenty and forty metres deep and though some enhance the riverside with mature trees, a number of treeless gardens reveal white stucco houses. The monolithic 1930s Thames Eyot block of flats is built on the site of the eighteenth-century Poulett Lodge. Although the balustrade, loggia and boat-house of the old mansion give the riverside a grandeur which matches the York House waterfront on the other side of Twickenham, the scale and design of the block of flats do not complement the setting. The effect has been exacerbated by a second modern block beside the Twickenham Embankment.

Twickenham Embankment retains a special character of brick and granite wharves backed by the attractive grouping of St Mary's church and the eighteenth-century waterfront of houses and pubs. The space is popular with fishermen, boat repairers, walkers and people just sitting enjoying the protected southern aspect and watching the swans, riverside activity and the view across to the boatyards on Eel Pie Island. Car parking, vandalised brick planters and graffiti-covered seats detract from the scene. The derelict swimming baths building is out-of-scale with the rest of the waterfront and introduces a rather bleak dead end to the Embankment. The site offers a rare opportunity to make new connections back to the centre of Twickenham and a potential location for expanding the surrounding civic facilities, such as the day-care centre, with fine views and access to the waterfront. This

could also be a good site for a relocation of the local library. If, in the future, the adjacent Thames Eyot were ever redeveloped and public access could be negotiated along the old balustraded waterfront, the embankment could really bring a new life and identity to Twickenham.

At the downstream end of the Embankment, the balustraded gardens of York House provide an example of how trees and public access could enhance the Thames Eyot site at the upstream end. York House, the offices of the London Borough of Richmond upon Thames, and its eccentric gardens create a fine foil to the busy wharves of Twickenham and the ramshackle activity of the boatyards.

The boatyards across the narrow forty metre channel on Eel Pie Island and the vessels on the river are an intrinsic part of the character of the area. It is rare to be able to watch a working waterfront at such close quarters without getting in the way. The enclosing trees at either end of the island and across the river in York House gardens complete the sense of containment. These wooded ends to the islands, as well as providing important wildlife habitats, hide buildings from up and downstream, helping to keep communities distinct and give the impression of a rural landscape. They have been designated as nature conservation areas, covered by white willow and sycamore dominant above a ground flora of tall herbaceous plants. The secluded woodland supports a good range of birds, including a pair of tawny owls, which can be heard calling at night. Townhouse developments on the southern side of Eel Pie Island detract from the rural character and could be softened by tree planting. The old bungalows on the northern side are gradually changing in character. The modest low wooden houses, set back in

26. Samuel Scott: *Twickenham Riverside* (*circa* 1760). Private collection

27. *Eel Pie Island* by Thomas Rowlandson.
Private collection

leafy gardens, are being replaced by two-storey brick structures with picture windows and concrete block garden walls. Eel Pie Island is the largest island between Teddington and Richmond locks. The wooded ends of the islands have been designated as nature conservation areas, covered by white willow and sycamore dominant above a ground flora of tall herbaceous plants. The secluded woodland supports a good range of birds, including a pair of tawny owls, which can be heard calling at night.

A tiny road weaves from the Embankment, under a footbridge in York House gardens, to the Twickenham Riverside, a picturesque grouping of white seventeenth and eighteenth-century terraced houses, surrounded by trees. The White Swan Inn sits in the centre of the group, above the old Twickenham ferry slipway. Viewed from Ham Street, across the water, this is one of the more charming scenes along the river. The distant bulk of the Regal House tower

block, visible over the tree tops, is the only intrusion into the skyline.

Historical background

Twickenham had a riverside settlement in neolithic times and achieved its identity as Tuiccanham in AD 704 when it appears in a Saxon charter. It is not mentioned in Domesday, since it formed part of the larger manor of Isleworth, but a church is said to have existed on the site of the present St Mary's by the end of the eleventh century. By 1635 Moses Glover's map shows the village clustering round the church, ringed with orchards and market gardens to supply the capital with fruit and vegetables. In addition to the Manor House opposite the church, new substantial houses were being built and York House can be seen in scaffolding on Glover's map with kilns working full tilt on site to supply bricks (see *plate 44*).

Nobility began to be attracted to the area in increasing numbers in the seven-

teenth century. Lord Cornbury, Clarendon's eldest son, lived at York House in 1661, Lord Bradford at Richmond House by the river and Lord Raby at Mount Lebanon. In 1720 John Macky could call Twickenham 'a village remarkable for its abundance of Curious Seats'. In 1710 John James had built Secretary Johnston a new house which Macky thought was 'exactly after the model of the Country Seats in Lombardy'. A few years afterwards St Mary's employed the same architect to make a stylish new redbrick nave in startling contrast to the sturdy ragstone fourteenth-century tower. Sir Godfrey Kneller, who was church-warden, organised the fund-raising. From the river St Mary's nave, with its pediment and portico, looks like another of Macky's 'curious seats' singled out for praise in fashionable Twickenham.

There were notable gardeners in Twickenham, who made their contribution to the area. Johnston, to whom John James dedicated his translation of Dezallier d'Argenville's work *The Theory and Practice of Gardening*, had, according to Macky, 'the best collection of fruit of all sorts of most gentlemen in England'. Batty Langley, who in 1728 wrote the highly influential book on *New Principles of Gardening*, was the son of a local gardener and worked at Twickenham Park. Although Whitton Park could not be seen from the Thames, the Duke of Argyll's mark was left along the banks of the river as he supplied his neighbours with many recently introduced trees from his large nursery. Walpole, who called him the 'treemonger' acknowledged that he 'contributed essentially to the richness of colouring so peculiar to our modern landscape'. There is an engraving by Woollett in which His Grace is seen in his gardening apron showing visitors around the arbor-etum. After his death many of the foreign trees and shrubs were transplanted to Kew by Lord Bute for the Princess Augusta and are still there today.

The Swiss artist J.H. Muntz made a view of the villas and gardens upstream at Cross Deep, where in the 1720s the Earl of Radnor had built a house by a backwater. When Walpole came to live at Strawberry Hill, he was scornful of his neighbour's eclectic garden buildings, which he called 'Mabland'. The Chinese temple has disappeared, but a gazebo, part of a bathhouse, from Radnor House garden, and a Gothic summerhouse from a neighbouring garden of Cross Deep House have been restored in what are now Radnor Gardens. Neither of the houses survives.

Twickenham achieved a character all of its own as a rural retreat that attracted poets, painters, actors, architects and musicians as well as courtiers and city men. Lady Mary Wortley Montagu, who moved into the area in 1719, found she could pass her time 'in great indolence and sweetness' with more freedom for cultural pursuits and more reasonable hours than prevailed in London with its nightly assemblies, balls and card-playing. Alexander Pope, who also moved to Twickenham in 1719, was largely responsible for its being known as the 'classical village'.

Pope's garden with its famous grotto was very influential on garden design and after his death inspired literary pilgrimages. Travellers looked eagerly for 'Twitnam bowers' and the weeping willows he had planted by the river. Catherine the Great is said to have requested slips from the trees for St Petersburg. An American made an exact plan of the garden and on his return laid it out with the Philadelphia highway standing in for the Thames. Pope's villa was destroyed in 1807 by an occupant who was weary of such persistent visitors but the underground grotto has miraculously survived though it is in urgent need of restoration (see *pages 65 -71* for a fuller account of Pope's garden).

In the early nineteenth century some of the large parks, notably Twickenham Park, began to be broken up and there was an infilling of smaller villas and cottages. Admiral Crawford in Jane Austen's *Mansfield Park* found a 'cottage at Twickenham' which he could improve with a gravel walk, a shrubbery and rustic seats. In 1807 J.M.W. Turner was able to design himself a Regency lodge in Sandycombe Road in sight of his beloved river. Charles Dickens occupied one of Aisla Park Villas for a time. Mount Lebanon was not broken up until the end of the century and some of the cedars which had given it its name can still be seen in the Lebanon Park estate. The land on which Whitton Park had stood was extensively developed in the 1930s and a few of the 'treemonger's' cedars are left scattered in Whitton today.

The advent of pleasure steamers brought a wave of day-trippers to stop at Twickenham ait, which became known as Eel Pie Island, recalling the local eel industry recorded in Domesday. Miss Morleena Kenwigs in Dickens's *Nicholas Nickleby* was taken there by steamer, to make merry upon a 'cold collation, bottled-beer, shrub, and shrimps', and to dance in the open air to the music of their travelling band. Dickens, who lived in Twickenham in 1838, had also tasted the delights on offer at the Eel Pie Island hotel, which more recently saw the early days of the Rolling Stones. The hotel has now been replaced by housing, an elegant pre-stressed concrete footbridge to the island having been constructed in 1957.

Twickenham's waterfront has retained its village appearance, but the selling of Richmond House and the building of swimming baths on the site, now unused, leaves the future of the historic waterfront to be resolved. Sir Ratan Tata's **York House** was bought by the Borough of Richmond in 1926 for use as council offices, after receiving its charter of incorporation. York House riverside garden with it remarkable statues, intended for Lea Park, Surrey, has been restored by the York House Society with support from the London Borough of Richmond and the Twickenham Society, adding to the varied interest of the delightful riverside walk to the old ferry and the White Swan. The slipway below the church, which, with the riverside road, is flooded at high tides, gives great character to the area. The working boatyards across the river on Eel Pic Island and the downstream view back to Walpole's 'seaport in miniature' from the footbridge, ignoring parked cars, has still the atmosphere of a Samuel Scott painting.

28. *The south front of Ham House* painted by Henry Danckerts (*circa* 1675, detail). Ham House, London

HAM

Landscape and natural history

The Ham reach curves from the edge of Twickenham to the edge of Richmond. Some of the most dramatic landscape features on the Thames are concentrated along this mile of the river. Richmond Hill and the wooded escarpment of Richmond Park rise above the lush flood plain of villas, meadows and avenues. The grounds of Orleans House, Marble Hill, Ham House, Douglas House and Petersham Lodge stretch down to the water's edge, uninterrupted by roads or suburban development. And the fine seventeenth and eighteenth-century architecture extends into the little villages of Ham and Petersham, nestled between the park and the river, and into Montpelier Row beside Marble Hill.

The panoramic view from Richmond Hill today sweeps over much the same Arcadian landscape which had such influence on the taste and designs of the eighteenth century. It is a view which has inspired painters and poets from around the world and raised such local feeling for the landscape that in 1902 it became the first view to be protected by Act of Parliament. From the top of the hill you can see the sun setting over the Chilterns.

Looking back from the river, the view glides up the Terrace Field to the strong line of the houses and the spire of St Matthias's church behind, along the crest of the hill. The broad hoggin terrace in front of the houses is an extremely popular viewing point, set below the level of the road with plenty of wooden memorial seats, beside a pub and protected by fine Victorian rods and bollards. A display board explains the view and some of the history of the landscape. The eighteenth-century line of pollarded trees has been replaced by limes and American oaks, many of which are dying, and a privet hedge has been planted on the front of the terrace. Although some trees are useful for shade, the division between the terrace and the field is best kept minimal.

The Terrace Field is managed for hay and wildflowers, creating a natural appearance which links to the water meadow below and in summer provides a popular hillside for picnickers, spread out on the long grass. The grassland is of only moderate floral diversity, dominated by meadow foxtail and cock's foot. Common wild flowers such as meadow vetchling, common vetch and bulbous buttercup provide some colour throughout the spring and summer. The grassland is managed by taking an annual hay cut in late summer, a regime which should encourage a greater diversity of flowers. Petersham Common lies on London clay but the steep slope assists drainage so there is less of a wetland influence on its flora and fauna. The common was almost completely open and bare of trees until well into the nineteenth century, except for some scattered trees and scrub on the lower slopes under the Petersham Road. At the top of the slope majestic oaks now tower above a dense and varied understorey containing ash, hawthorn, holly, elder and many other native shrubs. There is also a varied woodland ground flora including Lords-and-Ladies, enchanter's nightshade, and foxglove. A large clearing behind the Star and Garter Home is vegetated with tall herbs and this sunny spot is a favourite area for butterflies. Further down the slope, the woodland becomes rather more scrubby and is dominated by hawthorn and regenerating elm. The land is owned by the London Borough of Richmond but regulated and managed by the Petersham Common Conservators. Management largely involves periodic thinning of young trees and maintenance of the paths.

In winter, the hillside is a favourite tobogganing slope. The Terrace Field is enclosed by the Wick and the Petersham hotel to the south, and to the north, by the elaborate Terrace Gardens, a fine example of a manicured Victorian park. The Terrace Gardens are concealed within a frame of mature trees, but the lower section juts out into the Terrace Field, lining the path, which leads from the top of the hill to the river with chain-link fencing and the back of a shrubbery. Were the fence to be set further back to the north, where the ground drops away, it would be more discreet and the long grass of the field could continue under the trees. The straight path is aligned on Orleans House and with selective tree pruning across the river, it should be possible to glimpse both the Octagon and

79

HAM

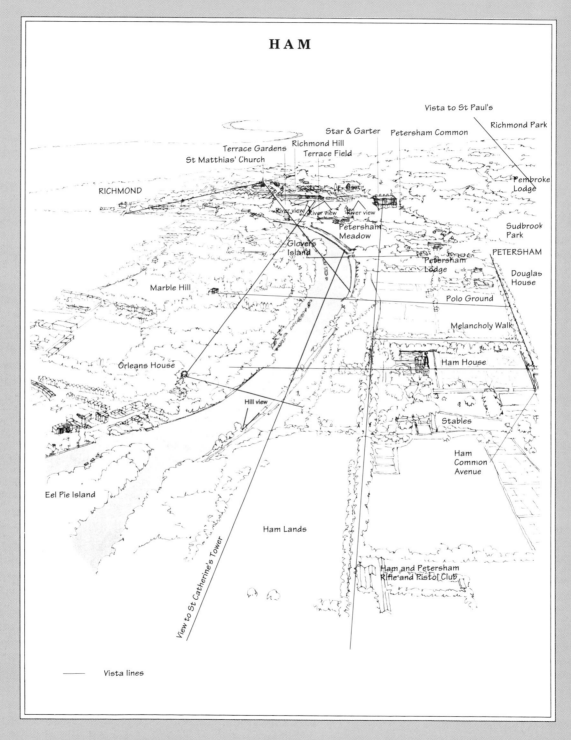

8

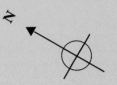

Vista to St Paul's

Richmond Park

Star & Garter   Petersham Common

Richmond Hill
Terrace Gardens   Terrace Field

Pembroke
Lodge

St Matthias' Church

RICHMOND

River view   River view   River view

Petersham
Meadow

Sudbrook
Park

Glover's
Island

Petersham
Lodge

PETERSHAM

Douglas
House

Marble Hill

Polo Ground

Melancholy Walk

Orleans House

Ham House

Hill view

Stables

Ham
Common
Avenue

Eel Pie Island

Ham Lands

Ham and Petersham
Rifle and Pistol Club

View to St Catherine's Tower

———— Vista lines

Marble Hill. Were the trees thinned, the public lavatories relocated and the concrete crazy paving and burnt-out shed at the bottom of the hill removed, one would also have a fine vista and route to the river.

Along from the Terrace, the Star and Garter stands out prominently from the wooded escarpment on the edge of Richmond Park. The home for disabled soldiers and sailors forms the eastern focus of the main Ham avenue. The mass of the huge red brick building is disguised by the oaks around its base. These trees are a critical part of the landscape frame, but where they have grown between Wick House (built for Reynolds to enjoy the view) and the Star and Garter, they have closed the view of the river painted by Turner and Rowlandson. Some minimal pruning could reveal the vista again without altering the wooded effect of the hillside.

Petersham Meadow sloping gently down to the river with cattle grazing on lush grass and wild flowers is still an amazingly rural scene within the capital. It shows how much of London's riverside would have looked as pastoral meadowland. The flora of the meadows is less diverse than it might be, following partial 'improvement' in the past, as is evidenced by the frequency of perennial rye-grass among the sward. A reasonable range of wild flowers is still to be found among the grasses, however, some of them in abundance. Bulbous buttercup produces sheets of golden flowers in spring and early summer, especially in the two smaller fields furthest from the river. The long grass is an ideal habitat for grasshoppers, while the flowers provide nectar for a good variety of common butterflies, such as meadow brown, common blue and small and large skippers. The meadows are owned by the London Borough of Richmond and leased to a farmer who grazes the land,

a regime now under a formally agreed Countryside Stewardship Agreement with the Countryside Commission. In time, this sympathetic management should increase the diversity of plant life, providing no fertilisers or herbicides are used. The larger field beside the Thames used to flood in winter until the 1950s when the low wall beside the towpath was erected. Although the field is still damp in places it would be very beneficial for wildlife to reintroduce occasional flooding. The grasses and wildflowers of the meadow form the critical middle ground to the view between the river and the hill. Broken fencing and a clumsy concrete flood defence wall around the perimeters of the meadow need attention. The disused waterworks beside the meadow could be dismantled and reinstated as a meadow. The white of Petersham Lodge gleams against the bright green of the meadow and the darker backdrop of cedars and the horse chestnut avenue which links the house to the river. The avenue has suffered over the past years and needs tree surgery and some replanting.

Once the grounds of Petersham Lodge, Petersham Lodge Wood is now managed jointly by the London Borough of Richmond and the London Wildlife Trust, with assistance from the Richmond and Twickenham Conservation Volunteers. The central avenue of horse chestnuts is flanked by many fine mature trees of which a colossal Oriental plane is the most noteworthy, being probably the largest in the country. There is little shrub layer, indeed meadow would be a better description than woodland for this place as there is prolific growth of flowering plants encouraged by the open canopy and the periodic flooding from the Thames on high spring tides. Spring flowers include lesser

celandine and lady's smock, while in summer these give way to sizeable populations of meadow-sweet and meadow cranesbill. Management of the site aims to maintain the historic central avenue and open character, while encouraging a shrub layer to develop around the edges. The embankment between the woodland and the river has been deliberately breached to facilitate flooding.

To the west of the land, woodland continues in a strip between the river and the grounds of a Sea Scout hut. This wet woodland, dominated by crack willow and grey alder, is much more overgrown, with a dense understorey of elder. There is lush growth of damp-loving plants, such as nettles, cleavers, wild angelica, Himalayan balsam and hemlock water dropwort. Similar tall herbaceous vegetation extends beyond the woodland in a narrow strip alongside the river, merging towards the west into drier, species-poor horse pasture.

The towpath becomes more open as it passes Petersham Lodge and Petersham Meadows and this is a particularly good place to watch bats on balmy summer evenings. Pipistrelle, noctule, serotine and Daubenton's bats hunt for insects over the river and around the trees. The many old buildings and large trees in the vicinity are valuable as bat roosting sites. During the 1985-86 London Bat Project 415 pipistrelles were counted at one roost in Teddington. The river banks along this reach are generally very good for wildlife, particularly adjacent to Petersham Meadows where there is almost a fen-like flora.

The Ham towpath is regularly inundated by high tides. The reinstatement of the east-west Ham avenue would present an opportunity to realign the inland footpath down the middle of the avenue on slightly higher ground, linking to the Petersham

Lodge avenue and providing a dry path for walkers when the tide is high. Invading balsam, elder and elm suckers along the river bank tend to catch water-borne rubbish. River litter collection has greatly improved over the last two years, but scrub control along the towpath would keep views open and reduce the problem. The sloping granite set banks covered in low vegetation are attractive and the stone steps are well used by fishermen. The River Lane slipway is extremely popular with boaters.

Behind the towpath and meadow, the village of Petersham clusters picturesquely to the side of St Peter's church. The fine houses of the village, set along a narrow winding road, are besieged by through-traffic to Kingston. The white wooden tower of St Peter's church and the red brick tower of All Saints' church stand out as landmarks against the wooded escarpment of Richmond Park. Further to the south of the escarpment, there is a glimpse of the white buildings of Pembroke Lodge. The Lodge has a public restaurant and a terrace with a fine view over the Thames Valley to Strawberry Hill. The Royal Parks are planning major improvements for the public use of this building.

Within the grounds of Pembroke Lodge, King Henry VIII's Mound offers both the magnificent keyhole vista of St Paul's cathedral, ten miles away in the City to the north east (*plate 33*), and to the south west down over Sudbrook Park and Petersham to the river and Marble Hill. Though the vista to St Paul's is now protected by government directive, the Mound is not well known, the view is not identified and the design of the space is disappointing. The Walk from Pembroke Lodge to Richmond Gate, designed as a viewing terrace when Petersham Park was recovered into Richmond Park, no longer has any views of the river. The Royal Parks and Crown Commissioners are currently reviewing the design of Pembroke Lodge Gardens.

Richmond Park, scheduled as a Site of Special Scientific Interest, has an undulating landscape and lies on the London Clay, with superficial deposits of High Level Terrace and River Terrace Gravels forming higher ground and Flood Plain Gravels and Alluvium covering some of the low-lying areas. This mixed geology and topography has given rise to a rich mosaic of dry acidic grassland, marshy and unimproved neutral grassland grading into more improved grasslands and bracken, with areas of woodland and numerous ponds and ditches. The park's acidic grasslands are the most extensive in Greater London and contain many plants which are rare in the capital. Scattered throughout the grasslands are numerous ancient oak and beech pollards, which support a large and unique assemblage of invertebrates, especially beetles, some of which are known nowhere else in Britain. Other rare beetles are associated with deer dung or are found in the park's wide variety of wetland habitats.

Unimproved neutral grassland covers much of Petersham Park (now part of Richmond Park), to the west of Pembroke Lodge. The sward is composed of a wide variety of grasses; hammer sedge is frequent and star sedge, which is very rare in London, can be seen in a few places. Harebells can be found, but generally the neutral grasslands are not particularly herb-rich. The Department of National Heritage, which manages all the Royal Parks for the Crown is drawing up a detailed management plan for the park, including individual specifications for each of the 486 ancient oak pollards. As much dead wood as possible will be left to encourage invertebrates.

29. *Swan upping in Twickenham* (*circa* 1840, detail) attributed to J.J. Chalon.
London Borough of Richmond upon Thames

Adjacent to and contributing to the extent of the park's grassland, Sudbrook Park golf course consists mostly of closely mown grass, but the roughs between the fairways and numerous mature trees provide some ecological interest. Traces of the great mound, pond and avenues can still be seen in the grounds and ideally features would be restored where they can work with the layout of the course. Management of the roughs with no chemicals or fertilisers and a late summer cut will help to maintain the habitats. Restoration of the stream and ponds would greatly enhance the nature conservation interest of the park. Appropriate planting of trees would contribute to a future generation of large trees.

Richmond Park connects to Ham through the wooded ride of Ham Common, opening on to the village green. The area immediately adjoining the park is mostly wooded and provides a valuable extension of the park's habitats. The remainder of the common is open, close-mown grassland bordered by trees. The pond has recently been dredged and supports amphibians. Ham Common lies on River Terrace Gravels which have produced well-drained, slightly acidic soils, and the whole of the common was once grazed heathland and acidic grassland. However as grazing declined from the latter part of the nineteenth century, the woodland of birch and oak has colonised. The fauna of the woodland includes purple hairstreak butterfly and a good variety of woodland birds. The green, with the village pond, is surrounded by fine houses and crossed by the southern avenue to Ham House. Gradual replacements along the avenue have affected its form and the whole line will need replanting within the next ten to twenty years. Interrupting white picket fencing and

adjacent boundaries and playing fields could be tackled at the same time. There may have been a mound at the Ham end of this avenue (see Rocque, *plate 18*), which if reinstated, would offer views through the recently reopened British Aerospace site to the river as well as forming a terminus to the view from Ham House.

Once part of Ham House grounds, the Copse and Holly Hedge field is now owned by the local authority. Relics of the old lime avenue can still be found along the northern edge of the field, as well as the old holly hedge which gives the field its name. Much of the field is dominated by cow parsley, but in one area theP delicate white flowers of meadow saxifrage can be found; it is a plant of undisturbed grasslands which is rare in London. The ancient oaks of the Copse, their trunks gnarled and twisted, form dense woodland stands in places, while elsewhere they are more widely spaced as wood pasture. The trees provide nest sites for many birds and probably bats, all of which feed on the large numbers and diversity of invertebrates supported by these stately trees. Many of the insects rely on dead wood. Until recently, the grass under the trees was closely mown, preventing the development of any significant shrub and field layers. This management has now been stopped, allowing elder, bramble and Swedish whitebeam to form a shrub layer. In one part of the Copse, ornamental trees have been planted very closely and now cast such a dense shade that nothing can grow beneath them. The trees could be thinned or removed to allow gound vegetation to reestablish and to encourage regeneration of the oaks.

Ham House and its gardens are being meticulously restored by the National Trust, within the walls of the property. The house's significance in the wider landscape

since the seventeenth century is marked by its lime avenues which extend across the surrounding flood plain. It is remarkable that such a network of avenues and vistas should survive within the capital. In addition to the southern and east-west avenues already mentioned, there are the remnants of Melancholy Walk, a long quincunx of trees between the eastern edge of the garden and the polo ground. The walk used to have raised pavilions and vistas across to Douglas House, originally the Ham dower house and now the German School. A further avenue survives from Ham House to Ham Lodge.

Ham House was designed to be approached from the river, but the waterfront has become something of a disappointment. The axial river avenue has been replanted, but intervening scrub and cherries block the view for much of the year and the disused lavatories across the water are an anti-climax as a terminus to the vista.

The public car park at the end of Ham Street further detracts from the scene. The bright gravel surface and glinting cars can be seen from miles around and disrupt the rural landscape character. The riverside car park is popular and offers an approach to the water for the disabled, but if the parking area were kept back from the water's edge behind low earth bunds and shaded by tree planting, it could be much less intrusive.

From the Ham House river edge, there are fine views to St Catherine's Tower, Twickenham Riverside and, in winter, to the Orleans Octagon and neighbouring Riverside House. Recent clearance has reinstated some of the connection between the gallery and the river, but there is greater scope for managing vistas through the gardens and reinstating some of the Regency setting. The walled garden of

30. *The Countess of Suffolk's House at Twickenham.* Engraving after Augustin Heckel (1749).
London Borough of Richmond upon Thames

Orleans House has become dominated quite recently by woodland, but has long had shrubberies much favoured by birds. In the late nineteenth century the owner, John Dugdale Astley, 'was not infrequently lulled to sleep by the rippling song of the nightingales, who never deserted the shrubberies'. Woodland birds, such as robins and wrens, are still plentiful. The sycamore-dominated woodland has little in the way of a shrub layer. The Orleans gardens riverside park has some fine waterside horse chestnuts, but the crazy paving paths, concrete street lights and vandalised benches are a disappointment. The rather neglected municipal treatment continues along the length of the Middlesex side. The raised river banks

have harsh engineered sides, chain-link fencing, sodium lights and a broad asphalt surface which contrasts uncomfortably with the rural gravel towpath on the Surrey side. In places riverside scrub conceals the river completely from the path. The London Borough of Richmond and the National Rivers Authority are experimenting with softer edges of willow and rushes along part of the Middlesex bank and the dense willows on Glover's Island help to screen the impact from Petersham Meadow, but the character of the whole path is inappropriate in such a distinguished landscape.

The urban character of the footpath is particularly intrusive along the Marble Hill waterfront. The villa was designed to be

seen from the river, framed by a stage set of trees, but riverside scrub and fencing obscure the park from the water. The villa has been restored by English Heritage and opened to the public. Marble Hill Park is very different from the grounds of Orleans House and is now a very well used public park with closely mown sports pitches, a cafe and a popular playground. In summer, concerts are mounted on the southern terraces. Mature horse chestnut trees and some fine old oaks and beeches edge the grounds. There are some small areas of limited wildlife interest beside the house where the ornamental shrubberies contain a few native shrubs beneath mature trees providing cover for one or two pairs of robins and blackbirds, the only such cover in the park. The reinstatement of the visual connection to the water and tree'd frame to the villa could complement contemporary uses in the park and greatly enhance the setting of the exceptional building in the wider landscape.

Downstream from Marble Hill, the developments at Meadowside and Meadowbank do not complement the surrounding villa landscape and though set back behind mature trees, they intrude into the view from Richmond Hill, particularly in winter.

Hammerton's Ferry provides a highly popular connection between the Surrey and Middlesex banks. This is the only ferry left in the study area and forms a much appreciated link for tourists and locals alike between Ham, Marble Hill and Twickenham. The viability of the ferry needs to be safeguarded, but the extent of associated moorings in front of the Marble Hill river frontage should be re-examined in the light of any proposals to reinstate the villa's visual connection to the water and the London Planning Advisory Committee advice on permanently moored vessels in front of historic buildings.

Historical background

The top of Richmond Hill, which has been called England's Frascati, has been a well-known viewpoint for centuries. By the 1650s a seat had been placed overlooking the view. A few cottages were developed on the east side of the road during the seventeenth century and in the 1620s a windmill was built on the site of the current Richmond Gate hotel.

From the 1630s onwards, the northern end of the Hill Common, on the slopes above the river, was granted out to tile-makers and a complex of tile-kilns grew up along the Petersham Road. Digging for clay made considerable inroads into what was left of the lower slopes of the common. The first improvement came about in 1700 with the laying out of the Terrace Walk with its double row of pleached trees, and the replacement of a group of cottages by substantial houses on the sites of 1-3 The Terrace. The Star and Garter tavern was built at the top of Petersham common in 1738 and the great era of development at the top of the hill followed in the decade 1765-75. During these years new buildings were added to the Star and Garter, 3 and 5 The Terrace were rebuilt, and Wick House (by Sir William Chambers for Sir Joshua Reynolds), Downe House, Ancaster House and The Wick (by Robert Milne) were all built.

The tile kilns were closed down in 1767 and the land was sold to the Duke of Montagu to extend the pleasure grounds of his house by the riverside. He linked the two parts of his grounds by a grotto tunnel under the Petersham Road and in 1786 acquired some more land when the remaining part of Hill Common was granted by George III and Queen Charlotte to Richmond Vestry – to become the Terrace Field.

The Star and Garter continued to grow during the nineteenth century until it became the most fashionable place for London society to visit for a day's excursion or for an evening meal. In World War I it became a hospital for disabled servicemen and was replaced in 1924 by the great red brick Royal Star and Garter Home designed by Sir Edwin Cooper. Below The Wick, on the hillside, a new purpose-built hotel (now called the Petersham hotel) was erected in 1864 to the design of John Giles.

In the 1870s the grounds of Montagu (later Buccleuch) House were extended into the gardens of the demolished Landsdowne

31. *A view of Richmond from the Terrace* painted by Leonard Knyff (*circa* 1720).
London Borough of Richmond upon Thames

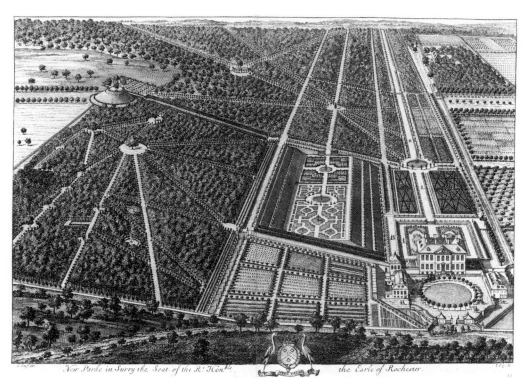

32. *New Parke in Surry* engraved by Kip (1708)

33. St Paul's cathedral seen from Henry VIII's mount. Photograph by Kim Wilkie

House and the entire hillside grounds were acquired by the Vestry in 1887 to become the public Terrace Gardens. In the 1930s Buccleuch House itself was bought by Richmond Council and demolished. Devonshire Lodge, another old mansion which stood by the Petersham Road, was also acquired by Richmond Council and demolished in 1968 and its grounds added to Petersham Meadow to improve the view from Richmond Hill.

The river valley beneath Richmond Hill, with all the elements of an idealised designed landscape, was captured to perfection by Turner in his view from Richmond Hill in 1819 (see *page 98*), the pale green foreground of the Petersham water meadows contrasting with the darker groves of 'umbrageous Ham', the wide silver-blue curving river with Windsor Castle (now no longer visible) in the distance and the villas shining through the trees. Goethe's romantic friend Pastor Moritz found the view unforgettable, 'one of the finest prospects in the world....Nothing I had ever seen is to be compared with it'.

Richmond's situation overlooking the curving Thames so impressed the American William Byrd, while he was staying with his friend the Duke of Argyll at Sudbrook, that he gave the name Richmond to the town which he founded in 1733 on the hill above the James River in Virginia.

Down in the valley, many eighteenth-century tourists commented that the little jewel of a Palladian villa, Marble Hill, gave the Thames a look of the Brenta. Built in 1724 for Henrietta Howard, George II's mistress, Marble Hill soon attracted a circle of courtiers and literati including Pope, Swift, Gay and Dr Arbuthnot. Amateur architects and garden designers had flocked to offer their services when the Prince of Wales advanced the money to build the villa. Colen Campbell's original plan was modified by Lord Pembroke and carried out by Roger Morris.

Lord Islay, later Duke of Argyll, of Whitton Park, who was one of the trustees appointed to take care of Henrietta Howard's allowance, gave expert arboricultural advice and a huge black walnut tree from his nursery, one of the largest in the country, can still be seen. Alexander Pope was 'the contriver' of the Marble Hill garden and he certainly would have advised on the sunken grotto, which has been partially restored by English Heritage. Charles Bridgeman was involved professionally and the garden, as seen on a survey of about 1750 had a green colonnade and a theatre, wilderness walks and quincunx groves, which can be compared with the conjectural classical retreat garden, from Castell's *The Villas of the Ancients*, with its hippodrome shaped green and semicircular arcade of trees. The Heckel drawing of Marble Hill in 1748 *(plate 30)* shows the neat stepped down effect as seen from a boat on the river. The house is still as described by Henrietta Pye in the eighteenth century rendered as 'white as snow' and stands out conspicuously in views painted from Richmond Hill. Missing from the river landscape now is the gothic barn designed by Walpole and his Strawberry Hill committee for the Countess of Suffolk, which at least one traveller mistook for a church.

The red brick house next door, built for Johnston, Secretary of State for Scotland, by John James, had a totally different appearance. All that now remains of the house is the baroque octagon, built by James Gibbs in 1720. Secretary Johnston entertained Queen Caroline in the Octagon when she was visiting by river from Richmond or Hampton Court. The greater part of the house, which later became known as

Orleans House when the Duc d'Orleans went to live there in 1815, was demolished in 1926 when sold to the Crane River Sand and Ballast Company. The Octagon and a small adjoining wing, however, were saved by the Hon. Mrs Ionides, who collected many prints and paintings of the area. On her death in 1962 she left the paintings to the local authority. The wing has been converted into a picture gallery adjoining the restored Octagon. Two hundred thousand tons of gravel were extracted from the site which has now grown into a wild woodland area, but there are still traces of the Regency shrubbery type of planting shown in a watercolour by Pringet.

Across the river, the setting of Ham House has hardly changed since Evelyn praised it 'as inferior to few of the best villas in Italy' with its gardens, groves and avenues 'on the banks of the sweetest river in the world'. Built in 1610 for a courtier at the time when Prince Henry was established at Richmond Palace, it was altered in 1671, the date on the urns surmounting the gate piers, for the Duke of Lauderdale, one of Charles II's most powerful ministers. Ham House has been restored by the National Trust and is still 'furnished like a great Prince's' as it was in Evelyn's day.

Walpole was dismayed by the walled-in, old-fashioned gardens, still in place in 1770. 'Close to the Thames, in the centre of all rich and verdant beauty, it is so blocked up and barricaded with walls, vast trees, and gates that you think yourself 100 miles off and 100 years back'. The National Trust has been able to restore the gardens to the seventeenth-century plan hanging in the house, making it, as the virtuoso, Roger North, saw it in 1695, 'one of the most beautyful and compleat seats in the kingdome'. The wilderness huts and the

cockleshell backed seats seen in the Danckerts painting showing the Lauderdales walking in the garden *(plate 29)* have been copied and tea can be taken in the original redbrick orangery. The avenues extending into largely unspoilt countryside preserve a strong feeling of Evelyn's day

Ham's 'embowering walks' along the river to Richmond are as rural now as when they were first extolled by James Thomson, who struck a new note in the appreciation of natural scenery. In Dr Johnson's words, 'the reader of "The Seasons" wonders that he never saw before what Thomson shews him' (see further *pages 95 -100*).

Petersham's 'smiling mead' is, in fact, more rural now than in Thomson's day as the old brick kilns have been removed. The Earl of Rochester's seat at New Park with its great vistas has now vanished and its grounds, known as 'Petersham Park' have been restored to Richmond Park. The mount, seen in Kip's engraving, formerly a standing in Henry VIII's chase, remains with its remarkable vista of St Paul's. The elegant eighteenth-century out-of-town houses entered from the Petersham Road, Douglas House, Petersham Lodge and Sudbrook Park still remain and their grounds, although mostly in recreational use, still keep the area green and free from development. John Gay spent much of his time in the Queensberry household at Douglas House, where his *Beggar's Opera* was rehearsed and trees were planted to celebrate its success. Much of his writing was done in the summerhouse, now destroyed, which his patrons built for him by the river. Sudbrook Park, styled as a villa in James Gibbs *Book of Architecture* and built by him in 1726-28 for John, 2nd Duke of Argyll, was probably planted with trees from his brother's Whitton nursery.

34. *Cholmondeley Walk, Richmond* painted by George Hilditch (1844, detail).
London Borough of Richmond upon Thames

RICHMOND

Landscape and natural history

Richmond meets the Thames in a characteristic leafy elegance. There are distinct 'gateways' to the town along and across the river. From upstream, the mown lawns and tall plane trees of Buccleuch Gardens mark a clear entrance, contrasting with the long grass of the open water meadow. From downstream, the brick arch of the railway bridge acts as a gateway from the open expanse of the Old Deer Park to the more formal enclosure of the palace waterfront. And from across the river, Richmond bridge acts as a magnificent entrance to the town, with the terraces of the new Richmond Riverside to the west, gigantic plane trees to the east, and the lively neon of the Odeon cinema straight ahead. Pausing on the bridge, the view downstream looks at the White Cross hotel, Asgill House and the succession of the railway, Twickenham and Richmond lock bridges. Upstream the view rises up the slopes of Richmond Hill to the Terrace and the spire of St Matthias's church. Though the towpath becomes more urban as it passes through Richmond, the substantial plane trees and small side parks continue the green corridor effect between Petersham and the Old Deer Park.

On sunny weekends, Buccleuch Gardens take on the atmosphere of a public beach. The south-facing lawns, sweeping down to the river's edge, are covered in deck chairs, rugs and sunbathers. This is one of the most popular spaces along the river, linked to the immaculate Victorian Terrace

Gardens above by a replica of Pope's Grotto, and by the towpath to the centre of Richmond. The footpath curves to the back of the gardens, leaving mature trees, simple grass lawns and uninterrupted river views to create a very successful public space. A few details could make things even better. The entrance from Petersham Meadows is abruptly blocked by a fence which is repeatedly torn down by frustrated walkers and the connection up to Richmond Hill is a gloomy confusion of concrete crazy paving, a burnt-out shed foundation and uninviting public lavatories (see Ham reach, *page 81*). The foundations of the old Buccleuch House provide an arcade and raised platform at the edge of the gardens where the deck chairs are stored. The structure could be adapted for performances and could house improved public lavatories. The banks of Buccleuch Gardens have recently been repaired with attractive wooden piling.

Between Buccleuch Gardens and Richmond bridge the waterfront is separated from the narrow Petersham Road by a row of attractive houses and hotels. Above the road, apartment buildings and the Poppy Factory rise up Richmond Hill, while below the Petersham Road houses and long gardens with tall trees create a shaded backdrop to the river path. A pub, canoe club, boatsheds and the Turk's Boats landing stage bring added activity to the extremely well-used promenade, but the standard of the paths, retaining walls, benches and little side-parks is disappoint-

ing. The pizza restaurant, tea and ice-cream kiosks could be more attractive. The large number of visitors and popularity of the waterfront deserve much better treatment.

Downstream of the bridge, the waterfront has been enhanced. As part of the redevelopment of the Richmond Riverside, the area has been opened as a series of sunny terraces overlooking the water. Controversy over the style of architecture aside, the riverside space is extremely successful with an exemplary quality of surfaces and furnishings. The brick and granite embankments, steps and slipways allow people to take full advantage of the river and spill out from adjacent pubs, wine bars and restaurants. The urban glare of the ranks of sodium lights at night and the incongruous wrought iron gazebo and restaurant marquee detract a little from the overall effect, but beyond, the White Cross hotel and the arched boatsheds in the base of St Helena Terrace retain the atmosphere of the old town, connecting back to the centre along narrow cobbled alleys. The arched foundation boatsheds have been echoed in the new development and are being used as workshops for building the traditional Thames wherries. Reopening boat storage in the arches under Richmond bridge would work well with the workshops.

From St Helena Terrace, Cholmondeley Walk skirts the edge of the old Richmond Palace. Fine old trees screen the

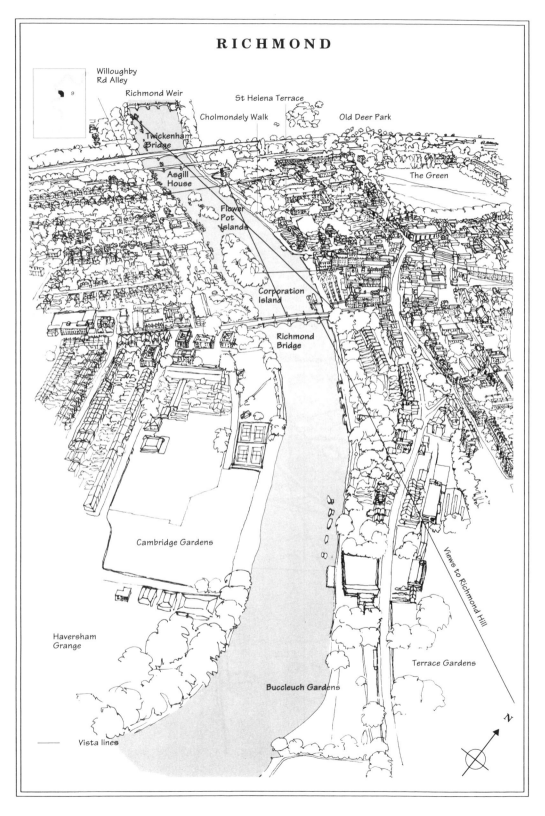

RICHMOND

Willoughby
Rd Alley

Richmond Weir

St Helena Terrace

Cholmondely Walk

Old Deer Park

Twickenham Bridge

Asgill House

The Green

Flower Pot Islands

Corporation Island

Richmond Bridge

Cambridge Gardens

Views to Richmond Hill

Haversham Grange

Terrace Gardens

Buccleuch Gardens

—— Vista lines

N

Queensberry House apartments and frame views of the Trumpeter's House and Asgill House. Paths connect back from the riverside to the Old Palace Yard and Richmond Green, creating an impressive sequence of spaces on the way to the centre of the town, with the exception of the bald area of car parking behind St Helena Terrace. On the path itself, shabby surfacing, vandalised benches and accumulated litter presently detract from the historic waterfront and alders planted between the towpath and the river will obscure traditional views.

The Middlesex bank, originally set with villas and their parks, has been gradually developed for housing. The fine modern architecture of Haversham Grange continues the tradition of villas set back between trees, but the brick blocks of Richmond and Richmond Bridge Mansions advance on the river's edge. The new development on Cambridge Gardens will have considerable impact on the Richmond bank. The asphalt path, sporadic rose beds, dried-out grass and municipal tennis courts do not at present make the most of what could be a spectacular waterfront promenade, looking across to Richmond and the hill. A new line of riverside plane trees would mirror the trees on the opposite bank and help to reduce the impact of redevelopment.

Below the bridge, the river bank is under pressure for redevelopment. Boatyards, houseboats and private moorings give a final echo of the old working character of the river, but they are struggling to survive against residential redevelopment. Though partially screened by the willows on Corporation and Flower Pot Islands, this bank is prominent in the view from Asgill and Trumpeter's Houses and the Richmond Palace towpath. Suburban housing can be glimpsed behind the thin river edge and thicker plantings of willows on the banks as well as the islands would do much to soften the view. Public access is squeezed down the unprepossessing Willoughby Road alley and kept back from the river. If efforts to save the boatyards ever fail and the bank is subject to redevelopment, building heights, river edge access and extensive waterside planting will be critical issues.

Corporation Island has a woodland of white, crack and weeping willows and also some hybrid black poplars. The banks of the island have reasonable nature conservation interest. Some of the stonework appears to be collapsing and when replaced could be designed to allow vegetation.

Flowerpot Islands are almost entirely covered by hard surfaces, with just one or two mature trees in the centre of each. However, mallards and Canada geese find them a convenient resting place, although disturbance by unauthorised angling prevents them from nesting here. It would be helpful to break up the hard surface to allow plants to grow and to assist natural regeneration of the trees.

Historical background

The manor of Shene, Richmond's Saxon name, was part of the royal manor of Kingston in Domesday, but was separated early in the twelfth century. At the beginning of the fourteenth century, the manor reverted to the Crown and in the second half of the century Edward III converted the manor house into a palace. Edward lavished considerable sums on the project; and his successor Richard II created a summer pavilion on an island in the river, but when his queen died there he had the palace demolished out of grief. A new palace, built by Henry V and Henry VI, was burnt down in 1497 and was rebuilt by Henry VII, who took advantage of the

Tudor peace to break from defensive architecture. This time instead of battlements he could erect gothic towers and pepperpot domes on his palace and enjoy games of chess and cards in the galleries around his riverside gardens. It was to this palace, an 'erthely and secunde Paradise', which, because of its 'wholesome airs' became the royal nursery, that Henry VII gave his title as Earl of Richmond and the town soon took its name.

Henry VIII used the palace frequently before he acquired Hampton Court and there were sumptuous pageants with jousting on the green and processions along the Thames. Elizabeth called it her 'warm winter box' – eventually taking refuge there to die. James I created a new park, now the Old Deer Park. His son, Prince Henry, planned a Renaissance court at Richmond with magnificent gardens but died before his ideas, which included a huge Pratolino-type grotto giant on an island on the Thames, could be carried out. Reclamation of the river front for the project had already been completed by Inigo Jones. The palace, which covered ten acres from what is now old Palace Lane to Water Lane, declined and Hampton Court rose in favour. It was sold off by Parliament in 1650 and the main buildings were quickly demolished. All that now remains of the once favourite royal palace is the original gateway into the courtyard carrying the arms of Henry VII and Nos. 1, 2, 3 The Wardrobe in Old Palace Yard. Richmond's fortunes changed in 1718, when the future George II and Queen Caroline made Richmond Lodge a royal retreat. An elegant terrace of houses was built for Caroline's Maids of Honour and other courtiers' houses appeared round the Richmond green.

Defoe greatly admired the area with 'houses surrounded by gardens, walks,

vistas, avenues representing all the beauties of building and all the pleasures of planting'. He feared, however, that its status and popularity would decline if the Court ever left. When this happened, later in the century, Richmond had established itself in its own right as a healthy, beautiful place to live in and a popular resort by river for Londoners to enjoy its chalybeate wells, pleasure gardens, concert hall and theatre. In 1744 Thomson's friend, the poet and physician John Armstrong, had extolled in *The Art of Preserving Health* 'Richmond's green retreats', where 'an hundred villas rise'. Richmond's dominant character is still one of residential elegance, based on its long connection with the court and the out-of-town world of wit and fashion. Its latest riverside development highlights the town's determination to retain the atmosphere of its elegant past. A complex of buildings, designed by Quinlan Terry in Georgian style, evokes a memory of Richmond's royal past. One, with its pediment and portico is based on one of Chambers's designs for a palace, never built, for George III in the Old Deer Park.

A pleasurable riverside promenade was made beside the Earl of Cholmondeley's mansion in the 1740s and in 1760 Asgill House was built 'after a design of Palladio' by Sir Robert Taylor. Asgill House was painstakingly restored to its original proportions in the 1970s by Fred Hauptfuhrer.

In 1774-77 Richmond bridge was built on the site of the old ferry, transforming the appearance of the town. Cambridge Park was developed at the end of the nineteenth century. Later, before the days of planning legislation, factories, a bus garage and an ice rink were built beside Cambridge's old house, which was demolished in the 1930s. The ice rink has now also been demolished and the site awaits redevelopment.

35. J.M.W. Turner: *Thomson's Aeolian Harp* (1809). Manchester City Art Galleries

JAMES THOMSON
AND THE 'MATCHLESS VALE'

P OPE'S description of scenery in his pastoral poetry paved the way for a more
romantic appreciation of nature, but James Thomson struck a new naturalistic
note – with immediate effect. In Dr Johnson's words:

He thinks in a peculiar train, and he thinks always as a man of genius; he looks round on
nature and on life with the eye which nature bestows only on a poet; the eye that distinguishes, in every thing presented to its view, whatever there is on which imagination can
delight to be detained, and with a mind that at once comprehends the vast, and attends to the
minute. The reader of the 'Seasons' wonders that he never saw before what Thomson shews
him, and that he never yet has felt what Thomson impresses.

The poetic muse had ventured out of 'Twitnam's bowers' and grottoes, walked in the
countryside, ascended Richmond Hill and liked what she saw.

Thomson arrived in London from Scotland in 1725 and soon became a member of
the Burlington set. He delighted in taking long walks and viewing the metropolis,
'Augusta', from the surrounding hills, particularly enjoying the view from Richmond
Hill. In *The Seasons* in 1727 he exclaimed:

Heavens! what a goodly Prospect spreads around,
Of Hills, and Dales, and Woods, and Lawns, and Spires,
And glittering Towns, and gilded streams, till all
The stretching Landskip into smoke decays!

After Thomson went to live in Richmond in 1736 he added a more detailed description
of the local landscape for the final edition of *The Seasons*, written as Pope lay dying in
1744:

Slow let us trace the matchless Vale of Thames;
Fair-winding up to where the Muses haunt
In Twitnam's bowers, and for their Pope implore
The healing God.

Not only was the 'boundless landscape' sweeping up to 'majestic Windsor' and
'royal Hampton's pile' to be enjoyed from Richmond Hill, but the varied rural delights
of the 'vale of bliss' were to be explored on foot:

Which way, Amanda, shall we bend our course?
The choice perplexes. Wherefore shall we chuse?
 .... Say, shall we wind
Along the streams? or walk the smiling mead?
Or court the forest glades? or wander wild
Among the waving harvests? or ascend,
While radiant Summer opens all its pride,
Thy Hill, delightful Shene?

Thomson's eulogy of extended prospect had its origins in empirical philosophy. Addison, who had sought to trace the sources of aesthetic enjoyment in the same way that Locke had investigated the Understanding, had stated in 'The Pleasures of the Imagination', published in the *Spectator* in 1712, that 'a beautiful prospect delights the soul'. He maintained that, like grand architectural concepts, 'unconfin'd prospects' would extend the mind. Addison sometimes spent summer months at Petersham, where his patron, Henry Boyle, to whom 'The Pleasures of the Imagination' was dedicated, lived at Douglas House. Addison was full of admiration for his kinsman's neighbouring New Park, where Thomson's 'pendant woods' were 'cut through by an abundance of beautiful allies, which terminating on the water, looked like so many painted views in perspective'. Thomson offered the reader of *The Seasons* an Addisonian 'calm, wide survey' of the works of nature with 'all that enlarges and transports the soul'.

William Kent illustrated the 1730 edition of *The Seasons* and combined pastoral imagery with Thomson's eulogy of extended landscape in an Arcadian scene where swains allow their eyes to 'roam excursive' with arms outstretched to a classical villa river landscape. A copy was presented to Pope, who was a good friend of Kent and Thomson, all three being closely associated with Lord Burlington. Kent's *Spring (plate 36)* shows a villa with an undercroft grotto and his *Autumn* has a domed villa with a Diocletian window and more than a hint of Chiswick.

It was the versatile Kent – architect, decorator and painter – who was to transform the new cult of perceiving beauty in landscape and the time-honoured pastoral tradition in poetry into landscape gardening, so that, in the words of Isaac Ware, 'what had so long ravished in the idea, now appeared in reality'. Artificial formal gardens having been replaced by Pope's neat simplicity of dressed nature, Kent, in Walpole's famous words, 'leaped the fence and saw that all nature was a garden', and at Claremont and Esher, two landscaped gardens referred to in *The Seasons*, he imitated nature's pictorial scenery as described by Thomson. 'Mahomet imagined an Elysium', wrote Walpole, 'but Kent created many'.

Kent and Thomson had the advantage over Pope of having made the Grand Tour and having seen the poetic conceptions of the mythological classical landscapes, painted by Claude and Poussin, in reality. The picturesque viewpoint added a new approach to

36. William Kent: Frontispiece for *Spring* in the 1730 edition of *The Seasons*

the appreciation of landscape, hitherto poetic or scientific. Kent worked with 'the pencil of his imagination' in his landscape gardening, according to Walpole, and in 'The Castle of Indolence', written at Richmond in 1748, Thomson, who became known in the nineteenth century as the 'Claude of poets', pays tribute to:

Whate'er Lorrain light-touched with softening Hue,
Or savage Rosa dashed, or learned Poussin drew.

Thomson was a formative influence on J.M.W.Turner, who called him 'the great poet of Nature'. Soon after he settled at Twickenham in 1807, Turner, who devoted much time to his 'Verse Book', planned to write a long lyrical poem on Thomson's *The Seasons*, which inspired much of the subject matter of his paintings. Turner, who adhered to the classical doctrine of *ut pictura poesis* (painting is like poetry), also felt a strong bond with Alexander Pope and his ideas. These Ruskin dubbed 'Twickenham classicism' and regretted that Turner should see fit to perpetuate the myth of Arcadian rural felicity. In his painting of *Thomson's Aeolian Harp* of 1809 *(plate 35)* Turner shows an idealised view of Twickenham with Pope's villa also included in the view. For this painting Turner published thirty-two lines in tribute to the creative genius of the two Augustan poets:

On Thomson's tomb the dewy drops distil,
Soft tears of pity shed for Pope's lost fane,
To worth and verse adheres sad memory still,
Scorning to wear ensnaring fashion's chain.

In silence go fair Thames for all is laid;
His pastoral reeds untied and harp unstrung,
Sunk is their harmony in Twickenham's glade.
While flows thy stream, unheed'd and unsung.

The tribute to Pope was all the more poignant since Baroness Howe, who became known as 'the Queen of the Goths', had recently demolished Pope's house, inspiring Turner's elegiac *View of Pope's Villa at Twickenham, during its Dilapidation (plate 25)*, for which he drafted the accompanying lines:

O lost to honor and the sence of shame
Can Britain so forget Pope's well earned fame
To desolation doom the poet's fane
The pride of Twickenham's bower and silver Thame....

Turner's most famous and evocative view of the area is *Richmond Hill, on the Prince Regent's Birthday* (1819),where the combination of the ideal and real scenes were brought to perfection; the pale green foreground of Petersham's 'smiling mead' contrasting with the darker 'forest-glades' and 'Ham's embowering walks', the wide

37. *A view of the Thames from Richmond Hill*
painted by T.C. Hofland. Private collection

silver-blue 'fair-winding' river with Windsor in the distance, and the villas just visible shining through the trees. 'He looked and Nature sparkled in his eyes', the great romantic painter said of Thomson's descriptive verse on Richmond Hill. To his painting, now in the Tate Gallery, Turner attached the lines (already quoted) from *The Seasons* which had coloured the vision of his own landscape: 'Which way, Amanda, shall we bend our course?'

A description of the view from Richmond Hill by the French American, Louis Simond, a disciple of William Gilpin's, who visited in 1810, complements Turner's painting:

You see a vast plain, and the Thames winding through its rich pastures, where cattle and sheep graze at liberty. Dark masses of tufted trees project irregularly on the shape of bays and promontories over a sea of verdure, with detached shady islands. Here and there the eye distinguishes an oak stretching out its vast horizontal limbs... As far as the eye can reach in an immense semi circle, the scenery, always the same, is ever varied. As the prospect recedes, every slight depression of the level sketches the nearest distance in a rich outline of edging tops of trees, upon the farthest, fainter and blue, till all is lost in the vague greyish haze of the horizon with some indications of hills.

Simond's Tour was published in Edinburgh in 1815 and Walter Scott's *The Heart of Midlothian*, published in 1818, echoes his description. The Duke of Argyll brought Jeanie Deans down from London to Richmond to plead with Queen Caroline to save her sister's life and the 'equipage stopped on a commanding eminence, where the beauty of English landscape was displayed in its utmost luxuriance'. The duke, who lived at Petersham, was, of course familiar with the scene, but, wrote Scott,

to a man of taste it must always be new...and looked on this inimitable landscape with the feeling of delight which it must give to the bosom of every admirer of nature...They paused for a moment...to gaze on the unrivalled landscape which it presented. A huge sea of verdure, with crossing and intersecting promontories of massive and tufted trees...tenanted by numberless flocks and herds, which seemed to wander unrestrained and unbounded through the rich pastures. The Thames, here turreted with villas and there garlanded with forests, moved on slowly and placidly.

The Richmond panoramic view, with its underlying unity and simplicity, was greatly admired by tourists even after the cult of the Picturesque had taken them to Wales and the Lake District in search of more romantic scenes. It was seen as 'elegant Nature', as it were one vast landscaped garden, where, what Defoe had seen as the 'private beauties' of the planting a century before, had blended together to form a harmonious whole, united by the Thames flowing through the scenery. It is greatly to be hoped that, even given modern pressures, the essential Arcadian character of the famous view from Richmond Hill can be retained and enhanced by the new Thames Landscape Strategy.

THE THAMES:
CRADLE OF LANDSCAPE
GARDENING

THE THAMES from Hampton to Kew provides not only a remarkable history of the art of gardening but still has examples of important historic gardens by the most famous designers in the country. Of the Renaissance gardens designed by Salomon de Caus for Richmond and Twickenham nothing can be seen and only the Mount of the great perspective forest garden of New Park remains, but Ham has been restored as an example of a grand seventeenth-century garden and at Hampton Court the Privy Garden is now being reinstated as a magnificent William and Mary stately baroque garden (see *pages 37-43*). The stretch of the river with Syon on the Middlesex bank and Kew, formerly part of Richmond gardens, on the Surrey side, remains an outstanding example of two eighteenth-century landscaped gardens united by the 'fair-winding' Thames. The royal Richmond gardens played an innovative role in the 1720s in the natural style landscape gardening, which was soon to become a national obsession, famous all over Europe.

Queen Caroline was the acknowledged patron of landscape gardening. At the time of the Hanoverian succession, when, as Princess of Wales, she had accompanied her father-in-law, George I, to England, a reaction had begun to the formal baroque 'princely gardens' condemned by Shaftesbury, Pope and Addison. Although the princess came from Herrenhausen, a truly baroque royal garden, she was determined to take up the new landscaping ideas and, in her own words, set about 'helping Nature, not losing it in art'. Princess Caroline was not in a position to indulge her gardening passion by reordering George I's royal palace gardens, but it was not long before she had a most promising landscape in which to try out the new ideas by the Thames at Richmond.

Having quarrelled with his father, George I, the Prince of Wales bought Ormonde Lodge in 1719 and, renamed Richmond Lodge, it became a royal retreat. The princess lost no time in calling a gardening conference to which Alexander Pope, who had just moved to Twickenham, was invited. By 1726 it was reported that Caroline had 'greatly embellished' the gardens and although the following year, when her husband became king, she had other palaces, and is most famous for the creation of the Serpentine in Kensington Gardens, she still spent much time and renewed her gardening activities at Richmond, which was given personally to her.

Charles Bridgeman, who had been on hand to carry out Caroline's instructions from the early days, became royal gardener officially in 1728. Pope probably met Bridgeman at the gardening conference in 1719, and recognised his considerable talents. In 1724 Pope wrote that he was 'of the Virtuoso-Class as well as I... and in My notions, of the higher kind of class, Since gardening is more Antique and nearer God's own Work, than Poetry'. Pope had contact with Bridgeman at Chiswick, Marble Hill and Stowe and in 1726 over 'a little Bridgmannick Theatre' in his own garden. Bridgeman, like Pope, realised that diverse elements could be brought together in landscape design to give contrast and variety, and that there was also a place for historical, literary and mythological associations. Like Pope's own garden, there were still formal elements, but Walpole, the historian of landscape gardening, maintained that although Bridgeman 'still adhered much to straight walks with high clipped hedges, they were only his great lines' and it was his 'detached thoughts that strongly indicate the dawn of modern taste'.

Richmond Gardens were still much as they were in Queen Caroline's days when Walpole came to know them in the late 1740s and it struck him that Bridgeman had advanced the gardening reformation by daring 'to introduce cultivated fields, and even morsels of a forest appearance, by the sides of those endless and tiresome walks that stretched out of one into another without intermission'. Count Kielsmanegge had also noticed this juxtaposition of wild land and formal features in the Richmond gardens:

Leaving this seat of contemplation you pass through fields clothed with grass; through cornfields and a wild ground interspersed with broom and furze, which afford excellent shelter for hares and pheasants. From this pleasing variety, in which Nature appears in all her forms of cultivation and barren wildness you come to an amphitheatre formed by young elms and a diagonal wilderness through which you pass to the forest walk.

The cornfields and 'wild ground interspersed with broom and furze' in a forest appearance (called Broomfield on the Rocque plan) had to be introduced in fact 'for the benefite of the game' in which it was said George II had much pleasure. Although not interested in the rest of his wife's landscape gardening activity, the king largely ignored it, thinking that the queen paid for it herself, but Horace Walpole relished the thought that his father, Sir Robert, had as prime minister transferred a considerable sum from the king's own purse to hers for the purpose.

William Kent was called in to erect the garden buildings, seen on the Rocque map, notably the Hermitage, the dairy house and Merlin's Cave for Queen Caroline *(plate 39)*. Merlin's Cave, a gothic house cum grotto with six wax figures including one of Merlin, was built in 1735 to house Stephen Duck, the thresher poet and his library. It had trees growing out of its thatched roof. Many political jokes were made about Kent's buildings and the king told his wife that she deserved 'to be abused for such childish silly stuff'. It is not recorded what George II thought of Caroline's fêtes galantes by the Thames.

38. Engraving by Chatelain based on Marco Ricci's *View from the Middlesex bank of Richmond Lodge*

The idea of the fête galante had come to England through the paintings of Watteau, who was himself in London in 1719, and engravings of his enchanting park scenes were soon available. Caroline's court, which was also enamoured of the pastorals of Swift, Pope and Gay, was invited to relive Watteau's sunlit world of picnics, minuets, coquetries and masquerades in the Richmond gardens. Lady Mary Wortley Montagu described to her sister in 1723 the miseries of Arcadia at Richmond in inclement weather:

You may imagine poor Galantry droops except in the Elysian shades of Richmond. There is no such thing as Love or Pleasure. Tis said there is a fine lady retir'd from having taken too much on it. For my part they are not all cook'd to my taste and I have very little share in the diversion there.

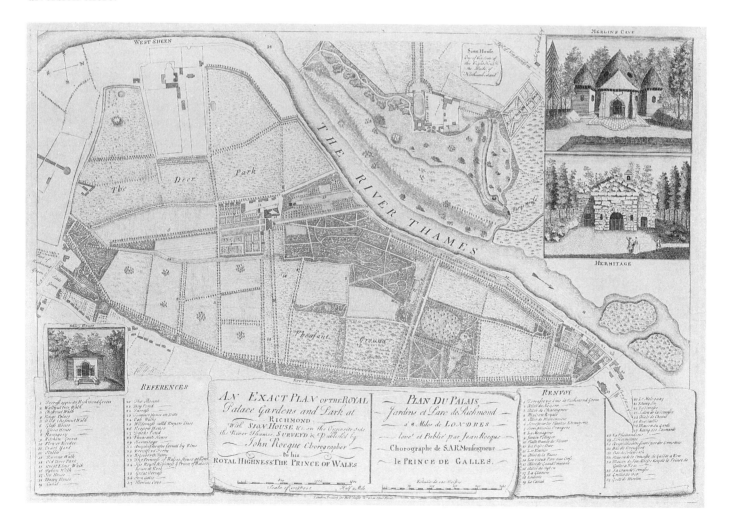

Fêtes galantes were out of the question for frail Pope, but he indulged in the masked 'Love and Pleasure' sensibility by epistolary amours with Lady Mary and through his pastoral eclogues with Henrietta Howard, who was George II's official mistress.

Walpole, whose own later Thames fêtes champêtres were much more comfortable affairs, delighted in the absurdity of the idea of the court and people of rank and fashion playing Watteau's game: 'a kind of impossible pastoral, a rural life led by those opposites of rural simplicity'. Lord Shaftesbury had already hinted at such behaviour in *The Moralists* as early as 1709, when he praised 'Things of a natural kind' rather than parading in 'the formal Mockery of Princely Gardens' and said: 'But tell me, I intreat you, how comes it that, excepting a few Philosophers of your sort, the only People who are enamour'd in this way and seek the Woods, the Rivers, or Sea-Shores, are yon poor vulgar Lovers?'

A striking example of the court imitating the simple life is the view of the royal gardens by the Thames engraved by Chatelain *(plate 38)* with unmistakable figures from Watteau's famous *Pilgrimage to Cythera*, which was also called *'une feste galante'*. George II, who is reputed to have said that he detested 'Boetry and Bainting both', could hardly have approved of such 'Love and Pleasure' mock-pastoral imagery, with his court playing at being rustic, in a view of a royal residence. It can be seen that the ferry from the Isle of Love from which the company were returning has arrived at Syon on the opposite bank of the river.

The gardens of Syon, at that time, as seen on the Rocque map of 1746 *(plate 18)*, were formal and square in contrast to Bridgeman's more naturalistic style across the river. On the 1754 revised Rocque plan there is a different scene. The Richmond gardens are unchanged but across the river at Syon the formal enclosed gardens have given way to lawns merging with the river scenery. This true natural style landscaped garden by 'Capability' Brown, highlights the two different concepts. The gardens of the Pope/Bridgeman style are sometimes called transitional as a step on the road to pure landscaping, but to their owners and designers they were not tentative but a positive style in their own right.

Brown's landscaping of Syon for the Duke of Northumberland was probably begun in 1753, soon after he went to live in Hammersmith. Hogarth's serpentine line of beauty, as at the Garrick, Walpole and Cambridge villas, is much in evidence in the shrubbery walk at the back of the meadow and in the waving ha-ha line. Brown departed from the Pope and Bridgeman theories of variety and contrast and rarely included associative features in his landscape gardens, relying on natural 'beautiful forms' to give satisfaction to the eye and mind.

Having been appointed royal gardener to George III, Brown was called in, in 1765, to alter the Bridgeman landscape garden at Richmond, and so had the

39. John Rocque: *An Exact Plan of the Royal Palace Gardens and Park at Richmond with Sion House etc. on the opposite side the River Thames* (1754)

opportunity of landscaping both sides of the river on the Syon reach. The famous raised terrace walk along the Thames from Richmond to Kew was removed and 'converted into waving lawns that hang to the river in a most beautiful manner', according to Arthur Young. George III's 'rural amusements' were a far cry from the mock pastoral fêtes his grandmother had indulged in. Farmer George had a grazing farm and dairy in the Old Deer Park with real shepherds to take care of the famous Merino sheep he introduced to Richmond.

Merlin's Cave, the Hermitage and the plaything dairy were removed, but the Richmond landscape was still enlivened by the Chambers ten-storeyed pagoda next door at Kew, built for George III's mother by Brown's rival, William Chambers *(plate 42)*. The two estates of Richmond and Kew, formerly divided owing to George II's feud with his son Frederick, Prince of Wales, were united when the Princess Augusta died in 1772 and George III moved to her White House at Kew and demolished Richmond Lodge. The idea of a new Richmond palace, which Brown's landscape had been intended to offset, was then abandoned.

The Richard Wilson painting *(plate 40)* shows the seemingly effortless Brown improvements to unite the two Thames landscaped gardens. The Arcadian scene, so beautifully portrayed by Wilson, was what in 1770 Thomas Whately felt to be the aim of 'modern gardening': an effect 'not sought for, not laboured' and with 'the force of a metaphor, free from the detail of allegory'. The gardens of Pope, Bridgeman and Kent with their associative links were 'emblematic' whereas gardens such as Brown's Syon, dispensing with the need for allegory, were, Whately felt, 'expressive' and suggested by the scene. The Thames has seen eighteenth-century landscaping along its banks from the early perspective vistas at New Park, the 'amiable simplicity' of Pope's garden and Marble Hill, Bridgeman's innovative Richmond and the mid century villa gardens of Walpole, Garrick and Cambridge; the culmination being Brown's treatment of its Syon reach, which happily, with no roads by the river, retains much of its original Arcadian character.

40. *The Thames at Syon*
painted by Richard Wilson (1760s).
Neue Pinakothek, Munich

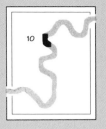

10

ISLEWORTH

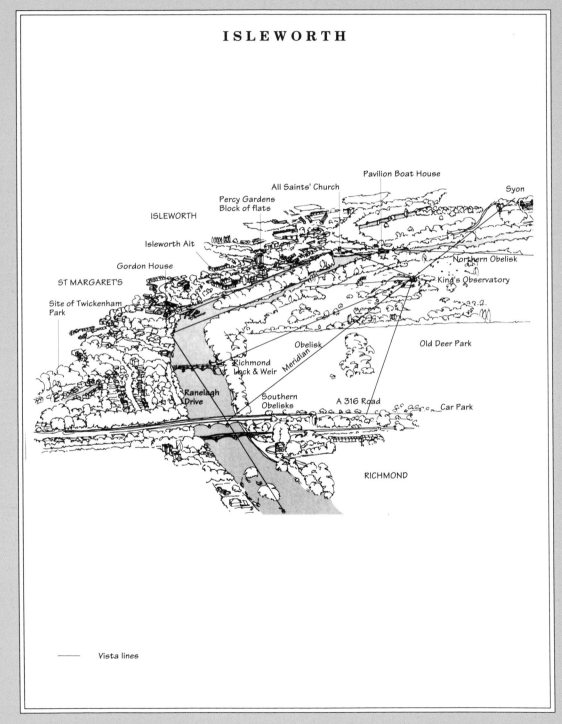

Pavilion Boat House

All Saints' Church

Syon

Percy Gardens
Block of flats

ISLEWORTH

Isleworth Ait

Northern Obelisk

Gordon House

King's Observatory

ST MARGARET'S

Obelisk

Site of Twickenham
Park

Meridian

Old Deer Park

Richmond
Lock & Weir

Ranelagh
Drive

Southern
Obelisks

A 316 Road

Car Park

RICHMOND

——— Vista lines

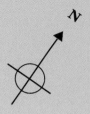

N

ISLEWORTH

Landscape and natural history

Isleworth, Syon, the Old Deer Park and Kew ideally need to be seen as a whole; a remarkable eighteenth-century parkland landscape with villas, palaces and riverside villages. It is only relatively recent management practices which have blurred the historical landscape continuum between the two banks and across the royal land from Richmond to Kew. The King's Observatory, which used to act as the focal pivot in the centre of the parkland landscape, has been gradually hidden behind a pen of scrub and planting. The original meridian has been completely obscured, although the 1778 obelisks still survive.

The Old Deer Park has evolved into separate compartments under tenancies from the Crown Estate. The southern third is leased for recreation and athletics grounds, divided between sports pitches, car parking, a swimming pool and a playground. The area beside the river is leased to the London Borough of Richmond. A group of beech trees and a playground sit in the middle of a broad expanse of close-mown grass, fringed by riverside trees. Four stone obelisks are set across the space, aligned with the King's Observatory. Scrub growth and conifer planting along the northern edge of the leasehold division is steadily blocking the view to the Observatory, isolating the obelisks, truncating the space and creating a harsh line across the landscape. English Heritage has amended the Register of Historic Parks and Gardens

to include the Old Deer Park in the Royal Botanic Garden Grade I entry, recognising the integrity of the whole landscape.

The southern edge of the Old Deer Park has been sliced by the busy A316 road, built in 1933 with Twickenham bridge, to create a new route out of London. The road, parallel to the railway, severed the connection between Richmond Green and the park. A pedestrian bridge over the railway leads off from the northern corner of the green, but the footbridge over the road is located down the other end of a car park. Beyond the car park, the space between the road and Richmond is an important area of trees and long grass, viewed from the road, the river and the railway. Twickenham Road Meadow is flooded from time to time, but a lack of management and past 'improvement' has led this fragment of old water meadow to lose much of its diversity. The north-western part of the site consists of the steep road bank with a slightly better range of wild flowers on the bank, including spotted medick which is uncommon in London. Reinstatement of this small relic of flood meadow with a hay cut would gradually improve the floristic interest. The ageing ornamental cherries on the northern side of the A316 have been supplemented with more substantial trees, planted by the Friends of the Old Deer Park and the London Borough of Richmond. A second pedestrian link to the park runs down a rural track and under an arch to the south of the road.

Coming into London, spectacular views open from the railway and Twickenham bridge, up and down the river, south to Richmond Hill and north to the Old Deer Park. Twickenham bridge could be cleaned and the railway bridge repainted. The King's Observatory can still just be glimpsed from the bridge in winter, though each year the view reduces. The Observatory is now surrounded by the Royal Mid-Surrey golf course, still retaining several mature trees, both scattered and in small copses. These include a number of magnificent oak pollards, which pre-date the golf course. The golf course is managed with nature conservation in mind, though more recent plantings of conifers and exotics detract from the effect. Several areas of thick cover, consisting of elder and willow scrub and stands of tall herbaceous vegetation, have been left between fairways to allow partridges and pheasants to nest in seclusion. The roughs on the golf course are remnants of the original acidic grassland, containing typical plants such as heath and lady's bedstraw, and also wood groundsel which is rare in London. Grasshoppers and butterflies abound, the latter including meadow brown, small heath, and small, large and Essex skippers.

The water-filled ditch, which lies between the Old Deer Park and the Thames towpath, is kept flooded by spring tides spilling over the towpath from the Thames. Along much of its length the ditch is heavily shaded by trees, and supports little aquatic vegetation. However, in the few places where sufficient light reaches the water, star-wort and Canadian pondweed grow on the water, while dense stands of great hairy willow-herb, yellow flag and many other water margin plants cover the banks. Coots, mallards and moorhens all find nesting cover in these areas, and kingfishers can often be seen. The willow-dominated woodland has been designated a nature reserve, and golfers are discouraged from entering. While a good variety of birds nest in the woodland at present, including tawny owls, the woodland and the ditch would greatly benefit from extensive management to create sunny glades; both the aquatic life of the flooded ditch and the woodland flora would flourish.

In the northern corner of the Old Deer Park recreation ground, an extensive area beside the flooded ditch has been left wild. The southern end of this rough area consists of tall herbaceous vegetation dominated by creeping thistle. The thistles attract large numbers of butterflies. Further north the ground is clearly damper, and a diverse wetland vegetation has developed, extending beyond the fence into the golf course. There is a wonderful array of colourful wetland plants, including the small-flowered yellow rocket – a nationally scarce member of the cabbage family. The London Borough of Richmond plans to maintain the diversity of this wetland vegetation by cutting the open areas on a three yearly rotation and coppicing most of the willows.

The gravel towpath from Richmond to Kew has a remote, rural character which is rare within a city. The informal gravel path makes an appropriate contrast with the paved surfaces of the urban waterfront of Richmond upstream of the railway bridge. Occasional benches have been vandalised

and might be repaired for those wanting to rest or linger on the long walk to Kew. On the remotest stretch opposite Isleworth Ait, dense woodland and the quiet river give the impression of being miles from anywhere. In fact sycamore scrub growth on both sides of the path has encroached to such an extent that in many places one can see neither the river nor the Old Deer Park and the view is restricted to a narrow tunnel of trees and the bordering stagnant flooded ditch. The northernmost King's Observatory obelisk has become completely overgrown by sycamore seedlings. Glimpses to the river and the Observatory would make the walk more interesting, bring light back into the stagnant channel and restore some of the historic visual connections across the landscape.

The Thames is fully tidal below Richmond lock, and expanses of mud and gravel are exposed at high tide. Well-established intertidal vegetation makes its first appearance in this reach. The river bank beside the Old Deer Park supports a rank, tall herbaceous community of docks, policeman's helmet, reed-grass and hogweed, which grow on the deposited mud and in the cracks of the sloping cobbled wall. The tree growth on the banks could be cut on rotation to ensure that there is always some tree growth but that no trees become over heavy and a danger to the stability of the river bank.

Richmond lock and the weir footbridge, restored for the 1994 centenary by the Port of London Authority in their original colours, provide an elegant link between the Old Deer Park and St Margaret's. The details of the footbridge are carried across into the railway bridge and the railings along Ranelagh Drive promenade, creating an interesting contrast with the rural towpath on the Surrey side. The railings

continue along the riverside walk as far as Railshead, broken only by a short stretch of aluminium barrier next to the Eel Pie Studios. The narrow riverside park is well used by students from the adjacent West London Institute of Higher Education, incorporating Gordon House. The views of the river, lock and Richmond Hill from the walk and park are gradually being obscured by ash and sycamore scrub growing out of the bank. A fine old cedar in the grounds of the former St Margaret's House acts as a focal landmark looking south along the reach from Isleworth.

Behind the riverside path, Twickenham Park has been replaced over the past century by the residential development of St Margaret's – an unusual collection of suburban houses of every style from high Victorian to Bauhaus.

At Railshead, boatyards and small factories reintroduce the working character of the river and continue as far as Isleworth, interrupted only by the private gardens of Nazareth House. These gardens block a significant stretch of riverside access which would connect St Margaret's to Isleworth and could eventually help to link a walk from Kew bridge to Twickenham on the Middlesex bank.

The river Crane joins the Thames at Railshead and extensive works are being undertaken by the National Rivers Authority to shore up the banks and enhance public access. The river Crane is tidal for approximately 800 metres, between the bridge at Northcote Road and its confluence with the Thames. The wildlife importance of the tidal section is derived not from its adjacent habitat (there is little of this since much of it is narrowly confined between the back gardens of houses) but from the channel and the fact that it is tidal. Several species of fish enter and

41. Isleworth riverside. Photograph taken *circa* 1930. London Borough of Hounslow

leave the channel with each tide and some fish may use the channel for spawning. The richness of the bankside vegetation varies throughout the length of the tidal section, depending on the type of bank; the upper and middle reaches are best. On the muddy banks, aquatic plants include celery-leaved crowfoot, water pepper and gipsy-wort. Although slightly less natural than the upper tidal reaches, the middle tidal

stretch is attractive, with its weeping and crack willow overhanging the banks, and many small boats moored at the ends of gardens. From Talbot Road downstream to the Thames, the lower channel has steep sides and in many areas is heavily shaded by horse chestnuts and sycamores. The river would benefit from the removal of some of the trees which shade the banks and water, and from management sympa-

thetic to wildlife by the residents who own the adjacent gardens. The bank sides should be adapted where necessary to support more vegetation.

The Duke of Northumberland's River enters the Thames a little further downstream in Isleworth through impressive stone arches opposite the northern end of Isleworth Ait. There is a particularly rich habitat immediately upstream of the high weir at its entrance to the Thames in Isleworth. A public path connects up to Silverhall Neighbourhood Park. The tree-lined walk and indeed the whole Isleworth skyline is interrupted by the Percy Gardens block of flats which stand out above the cluster of Isleworth roof tops. The river then passes through housing and a belt of sycamore woodland, also containing some fine beech trees, to the weir. Although the river is narrow, with restricted adjacent habitat, the riparian flora of its banks, particularly the northern bank towards the weir, is exceptionally rich.

Isleworth retains a distinct historic waterfront, enclosed down a side channel of working boats and barges much as at Twickenham. The tower of All Saints' church groups picturesquely with the Syon Pavilion boat house, the waterfront row of eighteenth-century houses and the London Apprentice pub. The stone embankment and old ferry slipway are popular with fishermen, boaters and drinkers alike. If the ferry were reinstated, it would provide a popular connection across to the Surrey bank and Kew Gardens.

Isleworth Ait, a large wooded island, creates a valuable heronry and screens the old industrial Isleworth waterfront from the Old Deer Park. The woodland is dominated by very tall sycamore and crack willow. The understorey of the woodland is mostly elder, but includes holly and haw-thorn. Ivy dominates the ground beneath the areas of horse chestnut, and, elsewhere, nettle and policeman's helmet form exten-sive and impenetrable cover. The side of the island facing Richmond has vertical steel-piled banks. The bank facing Hounslow is natural, though much of it is taken up by a boatyard and moored boats. At the north-ern end of the island, on the Hounslow side, an area of gently shelving mud supports a

small area of willow carr, dominated by common osier, which once provided the raw materials for the local basket-making industry. At low tide, mud and gravel banks are exposed on the Hounslow side of the island and at either end. As well as birds, the mud and shingle is also notable for its mollusc fauna, particularly the rare two-lipped door snail which enjoys life under debris which has collected here, and the equally rare German hairy snail. Many birds roost and nest on the island; bats can often be seen feeding around the island, and roost by day in boxes provided for them.

Isleworth waterfront has now largely been redeveloped for offices, pubs and flats. The hard edge, scale and some of the dock machinery have been retained though the uses have changed. Continuous public access, popular pubs, traffic and parking restrictions and well-maintained spaces have turned the waterfront into a low-key tourist attraction.

Historical background

The Old Deer Park contains much of England's royal history and contributes significantly to the landscape along this stretch of the river. Edward III first con-verted the Shene manor house into a palace in the fourteenth century and there was open warren for the chase all the way between Shene and Kew. Henry V, in the words of Thomas Fuller, then 'cut two great callops into crown lands' for building two religious houses (the Brigittine Sion convent opposite Shene Palace and a Charterhouse at Shene), to expiate his father's part in the murder of Richard II: an act Shakespeare made him ask his Redeemer to take into account as he went into battle at Agincourt:

and I have built
Two chantries, where sad and solemn priests
Still sing for Richard's soul.

There was a tradition that the royal founder's wishes had been that 'immediately upon the cessation of the service at one convent it should commence at the other and so should continue until the end of time'.

Henry VI made a small 'New Park of Shene' between the palace and the charterhouse. The charterhouse, a model of which by John Cloake can be seen in the Richmond Museum, was the largest in the realm and its building had been supervised by the royal comptroller as part of the 'kynges grete work' at the Palace of Shene. Its size can be seen on Glover's map of 1635, when it was still in royal use as stables after its final Dissolution in 1559. The Syon monastery on the Isleworth side had moved downstream in 1431 and the land was used by Henry VII for yet another royal deer park. Monastic lands were included in the land granted by Queen Elizabeth to Francis Bacon's family, who built a house there. The two sides of the river were brought back into relationship when Prince Henry was allowed to set up court at Richmond Palace and Lucy, Countess of Bedford, a favourite of the royal family, rebuilt the Bacon house in 1609. The countess laid out a Renaissance garden at Twickenham Park, complement-ing the de Caus work for the prince. Glover's map shows clearly that she had made good use of the old monastery canal in the garden design of her Twickenham park.

The prince's father, James I, did not forgo the sport Richmond had to offer and greatly enlarged the park on the Surrey side to over 370 acres by the addition of land once owned by the monastery and built a lodge in the middle of this 'New Park of Richmond'. It was after Charles I made the great new Richmond Park in 1637 that this park, which had provided sport for kings from medieval times, was called the Old Deer Park. King James's hunting lodge at the north-east end of what is now called the Old Deer Park was taken over by the Duke of Ormonde and made into a 'perfect Trianon' with a terrace garden. In 1718 Ormonde Lodge was leased to the Prince of Wales, who had quarrelled with his father George I, and renamed Richmond Lodge. It was here that his wife Caroline began her innovative landscape gardening, while still keeping some of the park as wild ground with broom and furze shelter for hares and pheasants for her husband's shooting and the southern part stocked with deer.

Following King George III's intention to build a new palace in the Old Deer Park, the houses in West Sheen (including that of the statesman-gardener, Sir William Temple), which had been built within the 'ample enclosure' of the Charterhouse, were removed. The palace was abandoned but the King's Observatory was built by Sir William Chambers close to the site of the cleared monastery in time for the observation of the Transit of Venus in June 1769. The Observatory as seen from the river is as fine as any of the Thames-side villas. The king's time for the Houses of Parliament and Horse Guards' Parade in London was originally set from the Observatory until Greenwich took over at the end of the eighteenth century.

The king continued to use Richmond

Lodge until 1772, when his mother died and he moved to the White House at Kew and had the lodge demolished. Lancelot Brown had been commissioned to design a landscape as the setting for the intended new palace. His plans are undated but improvements in progress were noted in 1765. The Old Deer Park, as seen in the more open part of Brown's plan, was later given over to George III's 'rural amusements' as a farmer. Part of the brick ha-ha, built in 1767 to keep in the king's new Merino sheep, can be seen along the Kew road.

Isleworth, once connected to the Old Deer Park by ferry, is first mentioned as a permanent settlement in an Anglo-Saxon charter in AD 695 as Gislheresuuyrth. It is then reported in the Domesday Book as having two mills, taking advantage of the river Crane. Medieval lords of Isleworth owned weirs on the Thames and the Isleworth weir had stakes at its upper end giving it the name of 'Railshead'. The Duke of Northumberland's river, as it was later called, was constructed in the 1540s to increase water power for the mills, when the manor was still in royal hands.

Before 1217 a large area of the present Borough of Hounslow was covered by forest, 'the Warren of Staines', which when cut down created the large barren tract of Hounslow Heath, which dominates the 1635 Moses Glover map. Wharves are mentioned in the middle ages to transport the products of Isleworth's water-powered industries, which progressed later from flour mills to breweries, calico and powder mills, whose dangerous cargo was taken to Woolwich. There was some agriculture in the district but by 1818 most of the open

fields were enclosed and market gardening displaced arable farming.

Isleworth housed some fashionable courtiers and men of letters in the eighteenth and early nineteenth centuries, but in 1860 Kelly's directory noted that Isleworth had declined when the Court left Kew and could never compete, in terms of fashion, with Richmond.

J.M.W.Turner lived for a time at the Ferry House, where he compiled his Isleworth sketchbooks with numerous river studies of the working landscape of ferries, mills, osier beds, fishermen, backwaters and wagons (see *plate 1*).

A new link united the two sides of the river a hundred years ago when the footbridge weir was built at Richmond lock, between St Margarets and the Old Deer Park. St Margarets House had been built on the river bank in the grounds of Twickenham Park at the Railshead end and in 1852 an estate, planned by the Conservative Land Society (a kind of political building society), was laid out in the rest of the grounds and extended into Twickenham. Gordon House, with its fine 1758 wing by Robert Adam, has now been taken over by the West London Institute of Higher Education.

St Margarets, which achieved its own railway station in 1876, predated Bedford Park as a garden suburb and had the great advantage of being a riverside site with its central curving roads backing on to a communal garden. The canal within these pleasure grounds brings the story of this area together as it is the one Lucy Bedford featured at Twickenham Park, still surviving from Henry V's first Syon monastery.

SYON

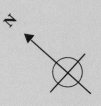

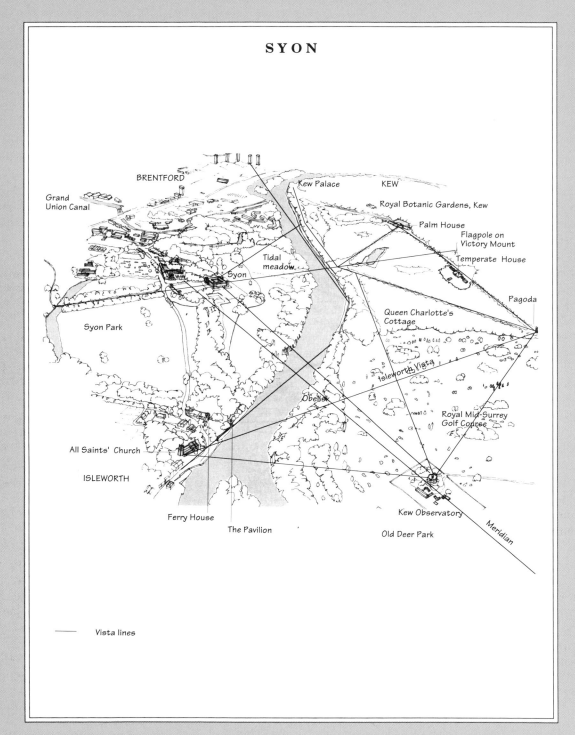

BRENTFORD

Grand
Union Canal

Kew Palace

KEW

Royal Botanic Gardens, Kew

Palm House

Flagpole on
Victory Mount

Temperate House

Tidal
meadow

Syon

Pagoda

Syon Park

Queen Charlotte's
Cottage

Isleworth Vista

Obelisk

Royal Mid-Surrey
Golf Course

All Saints' Church

ISLEWORTH

Ferry House

The Pavilion

Kew Observatory

Old Deer Park

Meridian

—— Vista lines

SYON

Landscape and natural history

The Syon reach is bordered by two of the most significant designed landscapes in Britain. Royal patronage at Richmond and Kew inspired some of the initial influential works of Bridgeman, Kent and Chambers. The current layouts of Syon and the Royal Botanic Gardens are still basically the work of Lancelot Brown and William Nesfield.

Syon Park is essentially a Capability Brown landscape. The ha-ha, water meadows and tree clumps survive, though advancing willow and poplar scrub growth have merged the clumps, obliterated much of the meadow and blocked views to the river. An aerial photograph from as recently as the 1920s shows the eighteenth-century landscape intact. The imposing house, with the lion silhouetted on the roof, is now only revealed by a single narrowing window through the scrub. The channels of the water meadow have become blocked and the clay land drains are steadily eroding away into the Thames.

The Countryside Commission, English Nature and English Heritage are currently working with Syon Park to reinstate the tide meadow, the Brown clumps and the visual connections to Kew and the river. Syon Park Limited has commissioned a landscape master plan to advise on the management of the historic landscape and the organisation of visitor facilities, parking and public access. This will set the guidelines for Syon's entry in the Countryside Commission's Stewardship Scheme.

The tide meadow at Syon Park, scheduled as a Site of Special Scientific Interest, is one of the few remaining Thames-side wetland areas. It is particularly unusual because part of the land is inundated twice daily by the tide. There is an interesting gradation of habitat from the river bank inland. In recent years, scrub has encroached on the heavily channelled intertidal muds. This is backed by wet grassland and reed beds which are also regularly inundated.

The scrub encroaching on to the riverside muds consists of a wide variety of willows and poplars, merging with historic clumps of lombardy poplar and swamp cypress. The shrub layer is not very diverse, being mostly elder, but the ground flora taking hold on the thick muds includes cow parsley and hemlock water dropwort. As the woodland is relatively recent, it would be beneficial to reduce its extent but keep some areas for roosting birds, particularly herons. The grazing regime will need to be adjusted to restrict encroachment of the woodland over the grassland areas. The creeks, which are a distinctive feature of the site, extend from the Thames well into the grassland. They are largely devoid of vegetation under the shade of the woodland canopy but are otherwise colonised by a large number of marsh plants, as described below. The reduction of the wooded area over the creeks will increase their floral diversity.

The meadow which is regularly inundated is dominated by reed sweet-grass but with a wide variety of other marshland plants also occurring. Marsh ragwort, yellow flag iris, marsh foxtail, water mint and meadow sweet are some of the flowers. The drier neutral grassland further inland is dominated by meadow-grasses, rye grass and species of bent. There are large tussocks of tufted hair grass in the transitional zone.

Apart from the tidal meadows, the long lake within the pastures west of the main entrance drive is important for nature conservation. Its margins are normally luxuriously vegetated providing good cover for many waterfowl. However, the lake has recently been dredged and it will be some time before the plants are restored completely. Great water dock, galingale and glaucous bulrush are all species of restricted distribution in London which are found on the lake edge. The surrounding pastures are closely grazed by cattle and are not of particular botanical interest as the sward is mainly rye grass. The proposed management for the pastures is continued grazing with no application of herbicides or fertilisers and this, in time, should lead to the development of a more diverse sward as the fertility drops.

One of the critical factors in the plan will be the reinstatement of the visual links across the river. Lines drawn on the plans of Glover and Kent show an awareness of important sightlines from at least the seventeenth century. The square of Syon

House is arranged on the cardinal points of the compass, to which later designs have responded. The north-south axis relates to the later meridian of the King's Observatory. The east-west axis, through the centre of the house, has been continued along the avenue towards Hounslow to the west and through the centre point of Nesfield's triangle of avenues in Kew towards the flagpole on the mount of the Temple of Victory to the east. Both the Syon and Kew avenues could be reinstated.

The significance of the visual links is also being considered by the Royal Botanic Gardens. Nesfield's triangle of avenues still forms the basic structure of the gardens, linking the Pagoda, Temperate House, the Palm House and the window to the Thames, with its cross-vista through the centre of Syon House. The lines of the avenues could be sharpened and the triangular framework made clearer in guides to the gardens, but the basic organising principle is still there. The relationship between the site and the outside landscape is less clear. The Isleworth vista, marked on the 1920 Ordnance Survey map between the Pagoda and All Saints' church, has been blocked by golf course planting and river edge scrub, as has the Isleworth view from the Observatory. The view from Chambers's Observatory to his Pagoda is being closed by conifers. And the views south from both Queen Charlotte's Cottage and Kew Palace have been obscured by scrub. The Royal Botanic Gardens are sensitive to prevailing winds into the site from the south-west and to the intrusion of high-rise buildings in Brentford to the north. For example, an office block across the M4 looms over the north-south Nesfield avenue as well as dominating the view over Kew bridge from the green. The westerly views across to Syon, as shown in the

Wilson painting and Turner's sketches, could however be reopened without affecting screenings to the north or south.

At the boundary between the Old Deer Park and Kew Gardens, the grassland beside the towpath is dominated by California brome, a North American species which escaped from Kew Gardens in the 1930s and is now common in many places in the area, particularly alongside the Thames. Pellitory-of-the-wall, another plant which has a restricted range within London but is quite widespread locally, grows upon the brick wall in the ha-ha forming the boundary of Kew Gardens. Another special sight along the towpath is the purple hairstreak butterfly. The oak collection in Kew Gardens provides abundant food for caterpillars of the butterfly. This species tends to fly high around the canopy, where it is hard to see, but it will descend to feed on the nectar of bramble flowers which are abundant along the edge of the path.

Growing in the tidal mud on the Richmond side of the river is a large stand of sea club-rush. This species is typically a brackish water plant, but the river water at this point is fresh at all times except when the river is exceptionally low and salt water can penetrate further upstream. Associated riparian species here include great yellow-cress, pink water speedwell and marsh ragwort, all of which are rare in London. A few plants of purple loosestrife also grow on the intertidal mud but this species is much more abundant on the bank top where it forms bright swathes in summer. The river banks on the Surrey side of the river have cracks and loose areas which have enabled plants to establish, making solid walls look considerably more attractive. A joint National Rivers Authority / London Borough of Richmond project, experimenting with willow spiling, begins in 1994.

The Royal Botanic Gardens at Kew has a global significance for its botanical collections. There are also some semi-natural areas, the most extensive of which is the woodland around Queen Charlotte's Cottage in the south west of the gardens. Oak is the main canopy tree, beneath which rhododendron provides cover for mammals and birds. Sheets of bluebells in spring are followed later in the year by quantities of flowers of two naturalised plants: perfoliate alexandera and martagon lily. Much of the grassland in the gardens has been re-seeded and treated with herbicides in the past, but some areas retain their original acidic character. Herbicides are no longer used on the grassland, and it is intended to return much more of the sward to its original character, especially in the arboreta. There are at least two bat roosts in the gardens, with several species of bats. Breeding birds include all three British woodpeckers, and spotted flycatchers, and the abundant bird and mammal life is preyed upon by sparrow hawks, kestrels and up to four pairs of tawny owls. Woodcocks, rare birds in London, are regularly seen in winter in the Queen Charlotte's Cottage grounds. Frogs, toads and newts all breed in a small marshy pond within the woodland area, and these provide food for grass snakes which were introduced to the gardens a few years ago.

The whole relationship between Kew Gardens and the river could also be improved. The gardens have effectively turned their back on the Thames. Gradually the riverside promenades of Bridgeman and Brown have been planted out. The site of the castellated palace and Queen Elizabeth's lawn have been turned over to parking and workshops (see Reach 12, *page 122*). And the river bank itself has

42. *A view of the wilderness, with the Alhambra, the Pagoda and the Mosque.*
Engraving from the book of William Chambers's designs for Kew (1763)

been reinforced with massive steep concrete revetments to meet flood threats of pre-tidal barrier days. The parking, infrastructure and protection of the botanic gardens are complicated issues and the sums involved in any reorganisation considerable. Over the next century, however, it may be possible to plan the future of the gardens not only as a world-class research centre, but also to take advantage of the exceptional character and riverside setting of the historic landscape.

Historical background

Syon's recorded history begins when one of Henry V's chantries, the Syon monastery opposite his Shene palace, was moved to the present site of Syon House in 1431. At the Dissolution the monastery was given to the Duke of Somerset, the Lord Protector, who built Syon House on the site with the materials of the abbey at the same time as he built his great Somerset House in London in 1547. The Protector of the Realm during Edward

VI's minority was king in all but name and even addressed the King of France as brother. In 1552 Somerset was overthrown and executed, one of the accusations of his opponents being that he had raised a great terrace around Syon House as a prelude to fortifying it. The manor of Syon, then forfeited to the Crown, changed hands many times before the lease was obtained from Queen Elizabeth I by the 9th Earl of Northumberland, whose descendants live there to this day.

43. Part of Moses Glover's map of 1635. Reproduced by kind permission of the Duke of Northumberland

Syon Park has always combined land-scaping by the best designers with a long-standing tradition of horticultural skills. The nuns had cultivated walled gardens and orchards and horticultural activity continued under William Turner, called the Father of English botany, for the Lord Protector. Queen Mary recalled the nuns temporarily but as Fuller records there was difficulty in reassembling the original occupants of Syon Abbey as 'most of the elder nuns were in their graves and the younger in the arms of their husbands'.

The 1st Duke of Northumberland, who took over in 1748, may have been re-sponsible for the demolition of Somerset's treasonable triangular terrace and the formation of a ha-ha. The formal gardens are shown in Jan Griffier's painting of about 1710 (*plate 4*) and are still there on Rocque's survey of London of 1744–6, but Canaletto's painting of 1749 shows that they have been removed. When Rocque's map of Middlesex of 1754 was published, the landscape is in place with a 'church Walk', a sinuous shrubbery walk leading from the house to the church at Isleworth. Payments to Capability Brown for one of his earliest commissions began in 1754 and a lake with bridges and Flora's column is described in the Syon entry of the *Environs of London* in 1761. In 1764 Brown worked, as royal gardener, for George III at Rich-mond Lodge, and was able to unite the landscape on both sides of the river.

Kew Gardens as we know them today are the result of the joining of the two adjacent royal estates of Kew and Richmond, formerly divided by Love Lane; ironically named in view of the animosity of the Prince of Wales and his parents. At Richmond Lodge the Duke of Ormonde had created long avenues from the house to the river and southwards towards Richmond Green. Queen Caroline was the patron of Charles Bridgeman and the new landscaping even before he was appointed royal gardener in 1728. As seen on the Rocque map, her Richmond gardens had an ornamental canal, a river terrace, forest walks, an amphitheatre, and diagonal wilderness. William Kent's hermitage and Merlin's cave are also shown (for more on Caroline's activities, see *pages 101-6*).

Capability Brown, commissioned by George III, broke up the Bridgeman avenues and formal groves extending the lawns to the river and letting in frequent views to the interior part of the gardens. He also demolished Kent's famous garden buildings. Richmond had always the advantage of the river, whereas William Chambers, working on the Kew landscape to the east had an unpromisingly flat and featureless site. As well as the botanical interest already provided for the Princess

Augusta by her garden adviser, Lord Bute, and William Aiton, Chambers relied on his garden architecture for inward-looking effect, erecting a mosque, an alhambra, a gothic cathedral, a ruined Roman arch, a Temple of Victory, a classical orangery and the spectacular ten-storey pagoda. In front of the White House, he created a lake with a white swan pedal boat, the 'Augusta', made for the future George III's seventeenth birthday.

When the two gardens were amalgamated in the 1840s, the lake was partially filled in and most of the buildings were removed. New entrance gates were erected on Kew Green when Queen Victoria opened the gardens to the public. The orangery and pagoda, a London landmark, remain as notable Chambers landscape buildings. The only Brown feature allowed to remain was his sunken laurel vale of 1773, now replanted as the rhododendron dell. The gardens we see today are the work of Sir William Hooker, the first director of Kew, and the landscape architect, W.A. Nesfield. The designs adapted to the new conditions and opportunities that the amalgamation of the sites, public access and scientific research brought.

Nesfield made the new Palm House, designed by Decimus Burton, the pivot of

his layout with a radiating pagoda vista, a vista of Syon, a broad walk and holly walk roughly along the old Love Lane. Nesfield's parterre round the Palm House was redesigned after his death in 1881, but his vistas remain. Nesfield had formed a new smaller pond in front of the Palm House from the original lake in the Chambers layout and in 1857, when the Temperate House was built, Hooker decided that the pits dug for the gravel for its terrace should be made into a larger, more natural, lake nearer the river, where Queen Caroline's Merlin's cave once stood.

The Queen's Cottage, like Kew Palace, is under the control of the Historic Royal Palaces Agency within the Royal Botanic Gardens. A *cottage orné* with a small menagerie was built for Queen Charlotte and the younger members of her family. Fanny Burney often mentions the queen's delight in retiring there, but when she took up residence at Kew Palace it was used as an ornamental dairy. In 1806 W.T. Aiton, who had taken over from his father as superintendent, was asked to design a flower garden in the paddocks of the cottage 'lately occupied by the kangaroos from Botany Bay'. It remained a royal enclosure until 1897 when it became part of Kew Gardens.

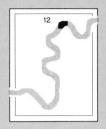

BRENTFORD AND KEW

N

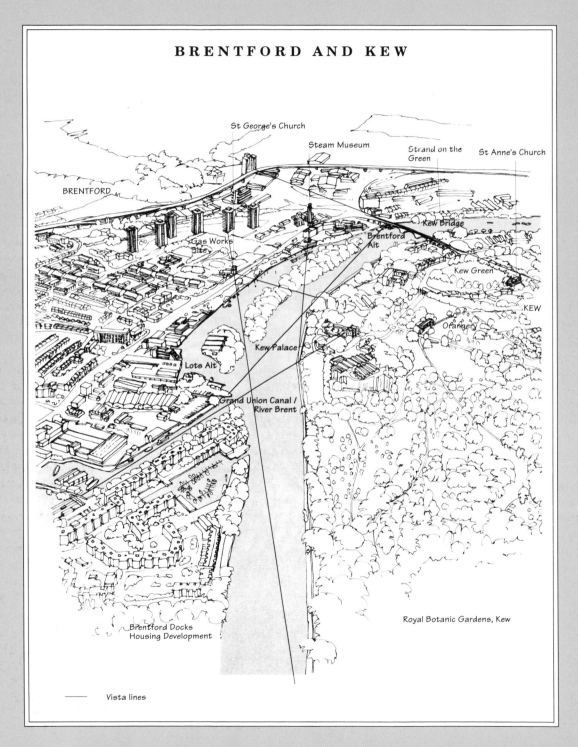

St George's Church

Steam Museum

Strand on the Green

St Anne's Church

BRENTFORD

Kew Bridge

Gas Works Site

Brentford Ait

Kew Green

KEW

Orangery

Kew Palace

Lots Ait

Grand Union Canal / River Brent

Royal Botanic Gardens, Kew

Brentford Docks Housing Development

—— Vista lines

BRENTFORD AND KEW

Landscape and natural history

Along the Brentford and Kew reach, between the mouth of the Grand Union canal and Kew bridge, there is a marked difference between the two banks. The industrial Brentford river frontage, though much run-down, still retains significant elements of its dockland past. On the Surrey bank, by contrast, the history of royal ownership has safeguarded the green spaces of Kew Green and the botanic gardens. The two banks are effectively separated by the thick tree cover of Brentford and Lots Aits.

The main area of the Brentford docks and railhead has been replaced by an extensive public housing scheme, built around the old mooring basin. As a major housing development, the scheme seems successful and, where large trees have been allowed to grow up along the river bank, the buildings merge into the surrounding landscape. But the open stretch of mown grass opposite the botanic gardens reveals a long three-storey façade which is not hidden behind a wooded ait and intrudes into the leafy setting of the gardens of Syon and Kew.

The northern bank of the Grand Union canal has retained a little more of the older industrial character of the area, though many of the buildings are now derelict and dock sides are covered by car parking or maintenance yards. Modern industrial sheds and security walls of a dark red brick tile have also reduced some of the

nineteenth-century charm of the riverfront. But the power of the locks and canal walls and the effect of the dilapidated corrugated iron dock shed at the mouth are still enough to evoke the identity and character of the old canal. The gas works beyond have now been demolished, but the yellow brick tower of the Steam Museum still rises over the area as a reminder of the energy of the industrial past.

The surviving industrial character is best appreciated from the water or the Kew footpath, as public access from the Brentford side is limited to short stretches of walks or historic slipways, such as Ferry Lane. The main walk, beside Corporation Yard, has been planted as a meandering path of scented shrubs. The walk has been vandalised and a more appropriate and robust design could fit the dockland context of granite, iron and brick.

At the foot of Ferry Lane, by Soaphouse Creek, a column marked the supposed crossing point of Caesar and one of Offa's councils. This made an intriguing reference to the long history of Brentford. At present the lane is a cul-de-sac and the column has been relocated to Brentford High Street. As part of a new linked waterfront path, the column could be restored to this remarkable spot.

The industrial waterfront now terminates in the Waterman's Art Centre, a thriving complex of theatre, cinema and galleries. A couple of wooden balconies have been extended out towards the river, but for

the rest the complex barely takes advantage of the view of the water and the wild, willow-covered islands. Window sills and walkway walls cut the view off too high and deprive the centre of an exciting relationship with the river. The heavy red brick and dark expansion joints of the building also look clumsy against the few remnants of nineteenth-century dockland architecture.

Beyond the art centre, Waterman's Park extends 380 metres along the river towards Kew bridge. The water's edge of granite sets, board-walks and open railings provides a good view of the activity on the river when the tide is in. At low tide, the channel drains to reveal an archaeology of boat and shopping trolley skeletons between the stately wooden dolphins. A few trees and the change in level help to protect the park from the worst effects of the traffic, while recent openings in the wall reveal glimpses of the river from the road. There is scope for making more of the dockland context. The Steam Museum tower, St George's church and the Brentford tower blocks – all now seen together in a rather confusing jostle of major landmarks – could be separately framed as viewpoints from the park.

St George's church has been converted to the Musical Museum. The Blomfield church now sits on the edge of the gas works development site but its river connections remain. It is aligned on a vista straight down the Kew/Syon reach between Lots Ait and the Brentford Aits, as well as across the Thames to the Kew towpath, from where it can still be glimpsed, framed between the Brentford Aits. The six tower blocks which now dwarf the church are visible from a great distance. They dominate many of the views from the Royal Botanic Gardens and the river itself. Interestingly in 1986, when the *Thames-side Guidelines* were drawn up, the gas cylinders were condemned as intrusive. Today they would probably be identified as part of the industrial character to be conserved. Perhaps the grouping of tower blocks may also one day be seen as an interesting part of the townscape.

Between Waterman's Park and Kew bridge the path is interrupted by a couple of private yards before ducking down into a tunnel of willow and balsam, serving a series of colourful houseboats. From across the river, the frontage of houseboats and trees does much to reduce the impact of new office developments. An effort has been made to vary the roofline of the new buildings, to use a brick stock which complements the yellow London stock and to retain the trees which mask the base and bulk of the development. A large disused six-storey factory still remains to be re-developed. The yellow and red buildings group together with the strong stone arches of Kew bridge, with the houseboats and trees, and with the Steam Museum tower beyond. The flat-roofed office block in bright blue and white on the Strand-on-the-Green side of the bridge jars on the scene.

Across Kew bridge to the Surrey bank, the character changes. One moves from the robust dockside of Brentford to the elegance of Kew Green, lined by trees and fine brick Georgian and Victorian houses around the cricket square and St Anne's church. At present the Kew waterfront does not reflect the elegance of the green. Arriving at the

Port of London Authority pier, visitors are greeted by graffiti, chain link fencing and stacks of rubbish. It is not until the Herbarium that the urban asphalt path softens to the rural hoggin of the towpath and the isolated municipal rose beds, benches and tennis courts revert to thick trees and native vegetation. Connections to the green are poorly signed back alleys. The houseboats, the willows of Brentford Ait, the Steam Museum tower and Kew bridge make a fine view looking out to the river, but the Kew waterfront itself is sadly neglected.

A road has been constructed behind high flood defences from Kew Green to a car park on Queen Elizabeth's Lawn. Parking is a continuing problem for the Royal Botanic Gardens and these spaces are badly needed, but there may be better locations along the Kew-Richmond Road which do not draw traffic through the green. The impact of the cars on the river is partly screened by the raised flood defences, but the severe engineering of the embankments from the water and the view down into the car park from the towpath do not contribute to the rural peace of the area. The steep concrete revetments support no vegetation and cannot be used by animals. The Royal Botanic Gardens have turned their back on the Thames. Queen Elizabeth's Lawn was the site of George III's castellated palace, commemorated in Turner's and Rowlandson's paintings, and the promenade along the river was a major feature of both Bridgeman's and Brown's designs. Kew Palace is now cut off from the river and the separation from the water deprives the gardens of one of their big assets.

The aits which divide the river into two channels form a significant buffer between industrial Brentford and Kew Gardens.

Lots Ait is a small island narrowly separated from the much larger Brentford Ait at high tide. It is dominated by a ruderal and scrub community which has developed from the osier bed which once covered the island. Lot's Ait provides an excellent opportunity for a variety of natural history studies. It has a special wild character of naturalised willows, rotting boats and gently rusting dock roofs. The slow progress of industrial decay into natural habitat has picturesque qualities as well as a philosophical resonance. Lot's Ait and the surrounding intertidal mudflats are of considerable importance for nature conservation. The natural character should be retained and it would seem inappropriate for any new development to be allowed on the island or mudflats. The largest area of intertidal mud habitat in the upper Thames is exposed at low tide around the islands. The muds have a rich invertebrate fauna including flatworms, freshwater shrimps and six species of leech. Twenty species of gastropod (mostly snails) have also been recorded and two of these, the ear snail and the trumpet ramshorn snail, have very restricted distributions. The muds are therefore a rich feeding ground for birds. Teal and wigeon visit the muds during the winter months, while other birds feed year round and nest on the islands.

The Brentford Aits (two islands connected at low tide) are similarly covered by willows and alder, creating a significant heronry as well as an important line of wild green in the river landscape. Again this woodland was probably once osier, but a variety of trees were planted in the 1920s specifically to screen the former gasworks. Many of the island's trees were felled and replaced by further planting between 1962 and 1964 because they were considered to be in poor condition. The severe vertical

44. Section of Samuel Leigh's *Panorama of the Thames from London to Richmond* (*circa* 1830) showing Brentford and Kew Palace opposite

metal camshedding could be improved by a more gently graded, vegetation-holding surface. Today kingfishers regularly fish from the willows which overhang the water, and the bird sanctuaries can be enjoyed by the public from the river banks without actual physical access. The aits, reflected in the dark water, form the major element in the views from Brentford, Kew and Kew bridge, disguising and revealing vistas to make the river seem larger and more mysterious.

Historical background

Samuel Leigh's drawing of about 1830 illustrates the vitality and contrast of this reach of the Thames. Old Kew Palace stands opposite a manufactory and there is a brewery across the river from Kew Gardens. The two islands, Lot's Ait and Brentford Ait, previously osier beds, had just been planted with trees to hide the view of Brentford gas works from Kew Palace. Osier beds can, however, be seen along the river, the willows binding the

bank and supplying the basket manu-factory. The Elizabethan traveller Hentzner had commented on the numbers of barges on the river laden with wicker baskets piled high with vegetables and fruit for London. For several centuries the area was important for fruit-growing and a whole-sale market was established at Brentford where London traders could meet local suppliers. Even when the Great West Road was cut through Brentford in 1925 it ran through miles of apple and cherry orchards.

Suburban development soon took over and there is little scope for fruit growing today.

The area at the delta of the Brent, which became Brentford Dock and is now built over, has traditionally been known as 'old England' owing to its immemorial associations. It was a Roman settlement in AD 1 and in 1929 a pile dwelling of AD 200 was excavated. It is an area of great archaeological importance. Excavations in the area bordering the Syon estate have yielded Stone Age tools belonging to passing hunters.

The Thames, curving from a northerly to an eastern direction at Brentford, cuts into the edge of a gravel terrace to expose a layer of workable fertile brickearth. The subsoil, recognisable by its vegetation, would have indicated an attractive place of settlement for the early farmers. A bronze sickle found in the area, now in the Museum of London, is a reminder of their activities. A large oak and bronze tankard, with a capacity of about four pints, found in the Thames, suggests that life before the Roman occupation of Brentford was not all

work but there was time for communal drinking feasts amongst the Celtic Catuvellauni tribe and their chief, Cassivellaunus.

Brentford is one of several places that claim Caesar's crossing of the Thames in 54 BC. Bede noted the remains of the palisade of stakes, cased with lead above and beneath the water, put up by the early Britons to guard a shallow stretch of the river. One such stake is on show in Syon House. Caesar mentioned both ford and stakes at the crossing in a statement in his *De Bello Gallico*, the first recorded piece of British history:

I led the army to the river Thames and the territory of Cassivellaunus. There is only one place where the river can be forded, and even there with difficulty. When we reached it, I noticed large enemy forces drawn up on the opposite bank. The bank had been fortified with sharp stakes along it, and, as I discovered from prisoners and deserters, similar stakes had been driven into the riverbed and were concealed beneath the water.

Whether or not Brentford can ever prove the claim to Caesar's crossing recorded on the memorial stone erected in 1909 (see *plate 2*), the strategic importance of the ford is unquestionable and is demonstrated by the Battle of Brentford between Edmund Ironside and Canute in 1016. The ancient ford over the Thames at the confluence of the river Brent, which had given the town its Saxon name, was replaced in medieval times by a ferry. Brentford became a river port of some significance at the end of the eighteenth century when the Grand Union canal linked it with the Midlands and, via the Regent canal, to London. The area was architecturally enriched when the Kew Bridge waterworks, built in 1867, erected its triumphantly elegant industrial standpipe giving Brentford and Kew an eye-catching Venetian campanile. The tower is now part of the Steam Museum.

The Surrey bank of the river has a totally different appearance from industrial Brentford. Today there is the same contrast between commercial development and landscaped pleasure grounds seen in Leigh's panorama. Kew first appears in documents as a tiny hamlet in the early fourteenth century and only began to be known when members of the royal family or courtiers went to live there to be near Richmond. Among the first were Henry VII's daughter Mary, James I's daughter Elizabeth and Queen Elizabeth's favourite, the Earl of Leicester. Kew first became a viable community at the beginning of the eighteenth century, when more houses were built and a small chapel, much enlarged later, was built on the green. Hitherto residents had gone to church at Richmond or by ferry to Brentford. Kew bridge was not built until 1758. Kew Green itself has changed little in spite of extensive surrounding development in the area between the two World Wars.

Kew Palace was originally known as the Dutch House and was built in 1631 by a merchant from Flanders. Its first royal association was with Queen Caroline who rented it in 1728 for the accommodation of her children. She was then living at Richmond Lodge. In 1730 Frederick Prince of Wales set up a rival court at Kew House, which had belonged to the Capel family. William Kent was employed to improve the house, which became known as the White House to distinguish it from the red-brick Dutch House. After Prince Frederick's death in 1751, the Princess Augusta continued to live in the White House until her own death in 1772, when it was taken over by George III. The Kew Palace garden was restored in the 1970s and a mount raised to view the river.

The White House was demolished at the end of the century when the shell of a new castellated palace was built by the river, only to be demolished in its turn by George IV in 1828. George III became increasingly confined to Windsor and Queen Charlotte only visited Kew occasionally, but as she spent the last five months of her life in 1818 in the Dutch House, it became known as Kew Palace thereafter. It is now managed by Historic Royal Palaces within the Royal Botanic Gardens, Kew. The gardens, evolved from the contiguous estates of Kew and Richmond, were opened to the public by Queen Victoria early in her reign.

hill & houses higher

46. *Richmond Ferry* by James Marris (*circa* 1770). Private collection

THE AUTHORS

Mavis Batey is President of the Garden History Society and has taken a personal and committed interest in the Thames Landscape Strategy from its outset. She shared the research and writing of the historical backgrounds to each reach with David Lambert, but found there was more to this than could be properly covered within the bounds of the report. The six essays and introduction that she has written for *Arcadian Thames* reflect some of her many diverse interests.

Henrietta Buttery is a Senior Countryside Officer for the Countryside Commission and chairs the Thames Landscape Committee. She took the lead in encouraging the various agencies to work together and it was largely through her support that the Thames Landscape Strategy became a reality. She is a Member of the Institute of Ecology and Environmental Management and by tapping the expertise of the London Ecology Unit she drew up those parts of the Strategy and *Arcadian Thames* that deal with nature conservation.

David Lambert is the Conservation Officer of the Garden History Society and a former chairman of the Avon Gardens Trust. He is actively involved in the protection of historic parks and gardens of both national and local importance. He was co-author with Mavis Batey of *The Engish Garden Tour* and has recently published *Parks and Gardens of Avon* with Stewart Harding and *Public Prospects* with Hazel Conway.

Kim Wilkie is a landscape architect with his own practice, Kim Wilkie Environmental Design. Based in Richmond, he works in Europe and the Americas and lectures at the University of California, Berkeley. The Thames Landscape Strategy originated with his ideas for a Royal Fine Art Commission exhibition in 1991. He co-ordinated, wrote and published *The Thames Landscape Strategy* with the assistance of Marco Battaggia and the authors of this book.

The full report is published as *The Thames Landscape Strategy: Hampton to Kew* and is available from Customer Services at the London Borough of Richmond upon Thames.

ACKNOWLEDGEMENTS

The publishers would like to thank the Thames Landscape Steering Group and Kim Wilkie Environmental Design for permission to use material from *The Thames Landscape Strategy: Hampton to Kew.*

Jane Baxter of Richmond Local Studies Collection and Gemma Hunter of the Orleans House Gallery have been especially helpful over photographs for this book, but we would also like to thank: Marco Battaggia, Simon Lace, The Earl of Jersey, Lord Lambton, Lucilla Phelps, Nicholas Reed, Peter Sapte, Eileen Tweedy and Rafael Valls.

Photographs for reproduction were kindly supplied by the owners of the works as given in the captions unless the source is noted below:
Front cover: Robin Briault
Title-page, plates 5, 9, 17, 19, 20, 22, 23, 24, 29, 30, 36, 39, 45, 46: London Borough
    of Richmond upon Thames
Plates 4, 43: Syon Park Limited
Plate 6: Giraudon/Bridgeman Art Library
Plates 7, 15, 16: © Lucilla Phelps ABIPP ARPS
Plates 11, 18, 31, 32, 36, 38, 42, 44: Barn Elms Publishing/London Borough
    of Richmond upon Thames
Plates 13, 28: By courtesy of the Board of Trustees of the Victoria and Albert Museum
Plate 14: Mavis Batey
Plates 26, 37: Rafael Valls
Plate 27: Museum of Richmond
Plate 40: Artothek, Munich

Cover illustration: *The Thames with Hampton church* (1874) by Alfred Sisley.
From the collection of the Earl of Jersey
Title-page: *The Thames at Twickenham* (*circa* 1730) by Peter Tillemans. Private collection

The publishers are indebted to Professor Mark Davis, Tony Kitzinger and Edmund Crawley for technical advice and assistance.

INDEX

Barn Elms Publishing, 93 Castelnau, London SW13 9EL

First published 1994.
This paperback edition published 2000

Text © 1994 Mavis Batey, Henrietta Buttery,
David Lambert and Kim Wilkie.
Maps ©1994 Kim Wilkie

Printed in Singapore by Craft Print International Ltd.

ISBN 1 899531 07 6

All royalties from the sale of this book will go to the
Garden History Society. Details of membership of the
Society are available from the Membership Secretary,
5 The Knoll, Hereford HR1 1RU

Cover illustration shows *The Thames with Hampton
Church* by Alfred Sisley (1874). From the collection of
the Earl of Jersey

Barn Elms has published two other titles which have close links to this
area of London.

ALEXANDER POPE
The Poet and the Landscape

Twickenham and Chiswick both feature strongly in Mavis Batey's
Alexander Pope: The Poet and the Landscape. The book is a
beautifully illustrated and superbly written account of Pope's life and
work and of his endless fascination with his own modest
garden with its famous grotto and the grander landscape gardens of his
aristocratic friends. It is highly recommended.

ISBN 1 899531 05 X   £25

THE STORY OF THE PRIVY GARDEN AT HAMPTON COURT

Written by Mavis Batey and Jan Woudstra this book both
tells the history of the garden and gives a lively account of the most
ambitious garden reconstruction ever undertaken. The book is full of
wonderful illustrations and will give great pleasure.

ISBN 1 899531 01 7   £4.50